H

5/12

LOST
BALTIMORE

LOST BALTIMORE

A Portfolio of Vanished Buildings

Carleton Jones

The Johns Hopkins University Press
Baltimore and London

© 1993 by Carleton Jones
All rights reserved
Printed in the United States of America on acid-free paper

The Johns Hopkins University Press
2715 North Charles Street
Baltimore, Maryland, 21218-4319
The Johns Hopkins Press Ltd., London

Library of Congress Cataloging-in-Publication Data
Jones, Carleton.
   [Lost Baltimore landmarks]
   Lost Baltimore : a portfolio of vanished buildings / Carleton Jones.
      p. cm.
   Originally published: Lost Baltimore landmarks. Baltimore : Maclay, 1982.
   Includes index.
   ISBN 0-8018-4607-2 (hc : acid-free paper)
   1. Lost architecture—Maryland—Baltimore. 2. Baltimore (Md.)—Buildings,
structures, etc. 3. Baltimore (Md.)—History. I. Title.
NA735.B3J66 1993
720 ' .9752 ' 6—dc20   92-43452

A catalog record for this book is available from the British Library.

Contents

Introduction

America's big cities are the ghosts of their own structural heritage, especially in the Northeast and Midwest. What has made them so is not a single villain at all, but instead the worldwide flight of mankind to his coastlines, the vast reshaping of homelands, the twentieth-century skyscraper orgy, and the compelling destructiveness of the freeway age. Why should we care, then, if our own environment has merely reflected the general inevitable?

The point may be that man becomes restless, at least cultivated man, in a world shaped wholly by the present. He must feel the past around him in order to shape the present effectively. We now know that modern architecture has too often been a relatively primitive shaping of cheap envelopes for expensive machines—packaging, in other words, almost a gesture, like dropping a tea caddy over a teapot.

These primitive structures, with their massive, unarticulated masonries, pitiable landscaping, dull colors, and sexless forms, are often luckily, if joylessly, neutral, ready to be decorated and contrasted with old forms and new art, like some barren, towered Italian town in 1300 *A.D.* It is magical how livable a dull modern building can become when it has preserved companions that hint of the past.

Sadly, Baltimore shares with other historic centers the erosion of its physical heritage, never, perhaps, in as drastic a form as Detroit or St. Louis or Boston, but still with major wounds. Baltimore business and government has traditionally used far too lenient a hand in shaping the city physically, except where capitalizing land or taxes for the city treasury or friendly powers has been concerned. The result has been that many a choice structure on the periphery of the inner city has gone to rack and ruin or been taxed or milked out of existence, while perfectly sound things have been bulldozed over in areas where land values and location counted.

No more deadly formula for historic structures could be devised. Fortunately, Baltimore *sprawled,* especially deeply westward along the prosperous trade routes to Frederick and beyond. It became large and low-density in an age that really wasn't used to this, and the sheer spread of things helped preserve the periphery. Evidence of this are the dozen or so hilltop neighborhoods within four miles of the downtown area, which remain more or less intact.

But we have been repeatedly stupid, and also unlucky. Fire has claimed scattered structures, like the fine Robert Cary Long design of St. Paul's Episcopal Church of the 1820s, and it has also chewed up buildings in batches. A fire caused by a lumberyard tinderbox in the midsummer of 1873 swept away a four block area off Park Avenue, including two interesting and imposing churches of the day. Losses, especially in mid-Victorian banking grandeur and the spittoon lifestyle, were vast in the 1,500 buildings claimed by the great fire of 1904.

Redevelopment has probably claimed far more of interest. The first major planned city development that came down hard on heritage, if we ignore the clearance of downtown city blocks of some note to build City Hall, the old Post Office and the City Courts building, was the Orleans Street–Preston Gardens development immediately following World War I. This "city beautiful" extravaganza took with it the terraced old warrens of Courtland Street, a whole hillside of elegant Federal architecture and domestic lore that was considered one of the most important neighborhoods in the country (politically and legally) in the decades before the Civil War.

The next great jag of clearance came in the late 1950s with the "Civic Center" and Charles Center projects, responsible for bringing down the veritable core of the old west side, turn-of-the-century city. Along with this scraping was a more or less continuous obligatto of urban-renewal bulldozing that began in the late 1930s and reshaped the near east and near west sides of town, punctuating them with characterless lowrise public housing and highrise slums.

Before these changes, Baltimore had been essentially the husk of a big Victorian city with an Edwardian girdle draped across its middle as a result of rapid rebuilding after the great fire of 1904. By 1920 or so, downtown had ceased to have any major residential impact, so there was no question here, as in New Orleans or Charleston, of salvaging major housing or sponsoring new dwellings. Not a single major new downtown structure was built between 1930 and 1950. At mid-century the city's Colonial past had wholly vanished and its Victorian masterpieces were decaying fast.

During this same period, we were scandalously careless with our heritage of isolated country mansions, many of distinguished design, that became marooned by close-in neighborhoods and institutions. Philadelphia saved many of them in a park system. We tore ours down—graceful "Montebello"; the chilly masterpiece of "Bolton"; our only Czarist palace, "Alexandroffsky"; and our finest Italian Revival remnant, "Wyman Villa."

When harbor renewal came along in the 1970s, it was a vaster affair than the wholly business-centered Charles Center idea. It reshaped the south side of the downtown in a staggeringly stagy and visual way. However it finished off virtually all the nineteenth-century downtown of iron fronts, warehousing, and docking lore that fire had failed to take with it in 1904. The planners of the 1960s must forever take most of the blame for the destruction of picturesque "Frenchtown" on the western side of the harbor and the magnificent State Tobacco Warehouses that were built to last 500 years.

No one remembered that the warehousing complex had received about $400,000 in state grants in the 1930s that were used to preserve its monumental (and unprecedented on the East Coast) testimony to antebellum commerce.

The preservation business and its history is filled with strange timelocks like this that are irony itself at times. When the Sumner Parkers, 1920s art collectors, were building their sumptuous imitation manor on the south edge of the Greenspring Valley, putting in authentic antique structural features hauled over from Europe, the great Gothic Revival barony of "Glen Ellen" was rotting a few miles away. In fact, some of the Glen Ellen furniture and one bay from the 1830s relic were incorporated into the Parker Mansion, now the Cloisters Children's Museum. When clearance was almost complete in the harbor, the city managed to save one facade and place it in storage, as if collecting a specimen for a museum, totally oblivious that the front was legitimate only where it was, in concert with others, as a loft for catching light deep into space. A substantial sum was spent recreating Robert Mills' "Waterloo Row" in the Baltimore Museum of Art in the 1970s. Five years before, the row had been knocked over and the millwork from the 140-year-old buildings used to build a wall for the wreckers.

This was not abnormal, but simply the sort of thing that went on. Much of Baltimore's building activity from 1945 to 1970 involved clearance, actions that were naively believed to halt the draining of the center city by making it more accessible to automobiles. The marketplace, however, disciplined construction to the point where no new office space was developed outside of structured renewal areas. Holes were merely punched into the urban corridors, where it pleased speculators and where retailing and residential living could yield.

There are many ways in which a structure can be dispatched. One of the least noted may be that it can simply *die*. This is apparently what happens to some outstanding things that have merely stepped out of the mainstream of need, places like Robert Gilmor's "Glen Ellen" that, as we will see, pioneered the home as a picture or storybook affair on the

American scene. Then there was Latrobe's great Exchange, simply beaten to death after adapting nobly to all forms of public and private abuse. These were simply places unlucky enough to have lived into flush times when adaptive use had yet to be born out of need. There was really no tremendous pressure or need to utilize the site, with these and dozens of other examples.

One continuing problem in Baltimore that has condemned many buildings or prevented recycling of others or made reinvestment of one sort or another impractical is the high cost of land traditional in the area. Why the city, with its generous spaces for expansion on about a 240-degree radius and its low profile construction, should have such tight land costs has never been properly explained.

At any rate, high costs have almost always been the case. The land under the relatively small Davidge Hall of the University of Maryland's downtown campus went for about $10,000 nearly two centuries ago. Land on Eutaw Place and in other posh urban locales fetched up to $400 a front foot or so around the turn of the century. A basic factor behind the destruction of the city's picturesque old central Post Office of 1890 was the reported difficulty in finding a new site for expansion. Government property people reported in the late 1920s that they could not find a suitable central location for a new post office for less than $1 million!

In some measure, this book must be a record of Baltimore architecture, if only the architecture that isn't. The city is well served indeed in having an up-to-date architectural guidebook as well as a distinguished general structural history published a quarter of a century ago. By adding the victims of time, a fuller record can be achieved.

However, no general archive of the record books and drawings of Baltimore architects and important buildings appears to exist, though efforts in that direction are being made by the local chapter of the American Institute of Architects. Despite efforts by the Society for the Preservation of Maryland Antiquities, the Maryland Historical Trust, Baltimore Heritage, Inc., and the Society for the Preservation of Federal Hill and Fells Point, no general medium for recycling deserving structures has ever been set up for the city. There is not even a central repository for prints and photographs of major import to Maryland, or even an index of holdings.

Even without these aids, one cannot help but be struck by the feeling that Baltimore's role in shaping American design has been somewhat severely underplayed. Overlooked has been our role in the perfection of the urban row house. Our Victorian masterpieces tend to be less identified with locale, more the sorts of things that could have been built anywhere than outstanding regional or local achievements, but there, again, they almost always manage to be absent from the history books on the premise that, we can only suppose, better, more important specimens have survived in other areas.

When Henry-Russell Hitchcock was putting the finishing touches on an introduction to *The Architecture of Baltimore* more than a generation ago, he wrote that no one could confine an account of the rise of any building type to Baltimore, not even the row house, in the way that the skyscraper is sometimes confined to Chicago. "Not even in what was Baltimore's greatest period architecturally, the first quarter of the 19th century, was it a center from which major influences went out to other parts of the country," he relates. Today we would not, perhaps, be so sure of this, for it is obvious, as it was not in those days when architectural history was dominated by study of the written record, that the overwhelming mass of American building has proceeded without much guidance from urban professionals.

Our structures have been shaped, as they were not in Europe, by the opinions of educated laymen, and it is perfectly conceivable that Baltimore, as a waystation of Eastern travel from 1800 on, as well as the commercial resort of Southeastern business, could very well have set in motion seminal currents of design, even if artless and unrecorded. The actual record is little known and may never be known very well for it is buried within what happened structurally in smaller cities in the second quarter of the nineteenth century, a poorly-studied historical arena.

While it is certainly true that Godefroy's St. Mary's Chapel of 1806 was too early and insignificant an effort to contribute a strong vector to the Gothic Revival of the next generation, Baltimore owners and builders just as certainly fostered the style when it appeared full-blown on the scene. Gilmor's great "Glen Ellen" was snatched across the Atlantic from its romantic prototype, Sir Walter Scott's "Abbotsford," practically before the plaster was dry on the original, and styled by Alexander Jackson Davis to others' plans. But the result, as W. H. Pierson, Jr., admits, was that "all the ingredients of the picturesque, in both the house and its natural setting, were intentionally combined in a single concept for the first time in American architecture."

No one in his right mind, confronted with the evidence in this study, could claim that our victims have been negligible. A "Glen Ellen" preserved, or even an "Evesham" saved, would have given Baltimore a Gothic period piece which it does not have, something to vie with New York's "Lyndhurst" or the Green-Meldrim House in Savannah and round out Maryland's museum of nineteenth-century building. There is something more than mere pride of place, however, in preservation, the fact that the voices of the pre-electric past are preserved there as in no other medium. Of course buildings are not Beethoven or Michelangelo and they are decidedly not what some of our wilder theorists of the 1920s thought them, instruments of social reform.

But they are wonderful civilizers. We do not have to be apologetic anymore for being catholic, for liking structures of all periods. At the same time, we cannot be too contemptuous of the presently beleaguered International Style, for all its pallid look and lack of regional or national identity. Today's buildings, prisons, hotels, offices, and hospitals may all look the same, but the point may be argued that they also looked the same back in the much-admired and unified Georgian period.

The feeling today in American life is that the great expansive urban building boom is beyond us—that the great challenge ahead is not preserving downtowns anymore, but

50-, 60- and 70-year-old neighborhoods that will be going downhill fast in the next decades. The long term, then, hints at *more* rather than *less* attention to adaptive uses and preservation. Senseless razings seem to be behind us, but intelligent mastery of our environment still eludes designers. The American of the 1990s has lost his faith in modern design while he has lost, too, perhaps to his gain, that snobbishness about buildings that marred thinking of the 1930s generation and claimed so many helpless victims, particularly Victorian masterpieces of design. The thought occurs that perhaps with the modern world's absolute retrievability of information, its incredible flexibility of image, our "museums without walls," our ability to conjure the historic, at least in mood, that it may be the eclectic architecture of our past, the "Golden City" idea, that may be a more rational and representative style than the single-minded Buck Rogersism that dominated establishment architecture for at least a half century following the 1920s.

At the very least, a look at what we once had, some of it distressingly long forgotten, may redress some of the balance in favor of our eclectic and loving designers of centuries past. It can explain, in part, why we live in a sort of half-environment of our past—one that only care and year-round vigilance can keep from becoming hapless once again.

LOST
BALTIMORE

The Colonial Remnant

I t would be a rash soul who would claim any great distinction for Baltimore's Colonial architecture. Unlike Annapolis, which was at once a government center and a focus of Bay society, there was little need for anything that was not prosaic and work-related.

It was not a dull architecture, however. There was always, unaccountably, a sort of fun element. Where else would a courthouse be stranded on stilts of dirt, high above the town, when a street was cut through, instead of being relocated or abandoned? Where else would the citizenry, as they did in the 1750s, build a town wall as protection against Indian raiders and outlaws and then, during a couple of briskly chilly winters, tear down said fence bit by bit to stoke house and cabin fires?

There was a haphazard, almost fun-like note to the city's Colonial architecture as we know it from old drawings and photographs. It was uniformly free of pretentious notes. Even the largest late Georgian townhouses had a fine sobriety about them, and virtually all had some sort of mercantile or tradesman's work space on the first floor or cellar area, or both. The now-restored Robert Long House in Fells Point is a rare survival and illustration of the typical mercantile mold. Corner lots were almost universally used at least in part for business purposes, a mode of design that was to be preserved for about 200 years in the form of the "ma and pa" corner stores still extant in the city's more modest neighborhoods.

An Irishman named Fottrell appears to have built the first real brick home, one with freestone corners, about ten years after the town got underway. This 1741 structure was sited on the northwest corner of Fayette and Calvert Streets, a crossroads that was to see virtually all of Baltimore's urban history pass by, including documented visits of the great and infamous—John Wilkes Booth, Charles Dickens, Washington Irving, and hundreds of other celebrities.

Neither this home, nor any other built in its era, appears to have had any innovative note or influence from which a Baltimore architecture, even a Baltimore vernacular of itself can be said to stem. Fine local mansions like Mount Clare were really a part of Tidewater architectural tradition. Little frame dependencies like Baltimore's first post office were like a thousand others built all over the Colonies. Congress Hall, virtually a twin of the larger townhouses of Philadelphia, lacked any original notes.

What was original was pretty spontaneous and enforced to a large degree by Baltimore's site, far hillier than it appears today in the center city area. This accounts for the tumblesome look of old Liberty Street, the jumble of Federal Hill's slopes, or the jackstraw design, like some stage set, of the historic "Carpet Loom" building. In the pre-paving era, there was only one way to gain access to a group of hillocks like the Baltimore site: cut-and-fill and the driving of streets through deep cuts that were only rarely revetted and landscaped and universally muddy and at times impassable in rains. Such sunken roads gave areas like the midsection of Charles Street and North Calvert Street a quite different appearance in the Colonial period, as well as a different elevation, from what we know today.

If there is any sort of typical Baltimore structure of the period, one would have to say that it is the inn. These big ordinaries were at once a convenience and a hint of what the town was to become, a dominant crossroads. It simply was more accessible from land and as a central loading point than its rivals like Chestertown, Alexandria, or Georgetown, or even (late in the century) Annapolis.

One is struck by the individuality of these taverns, and the fact is that they run quite a gamut of formats. The Fountain Inn and several other imposing early inns were coaching inns in styling, with central courtyards and stables, designed as the termini of stage lines, well established by the Revolutionary period. Others, like the gorgeous General Wayne, appear more as urban hotels and social centers on the order of Alexandria's Gadsby's Tavern. Still others, like humble Kaminsky's, look like frontier inns that might have graced the Erie Canal, the Natchez Trace, or the Cumberland Road.

We must not forget that in practical commercial terms Baltimore acted for many years like a satellite of Philadelphia, and that its earliest architectural specimens unquestionably reflected what had been done in the older city, especially in regard to mercantile and shipbuilding architecture.

Two things are certain. One is that Baltimore's architectural debut was topheavy with the practical and with structures of truly "occasional" character. Of perhaps thousands of structures put up before 1800, only a handful have survived in unaltered condition. Then, too, because the Colonies were diverse and their surviving buildings from the earliest days are relatively representative, the destruction of Colonial Baltimore cannot be staged as some major disaster, although the town certainly offered fascinations of unpretentious sorts.

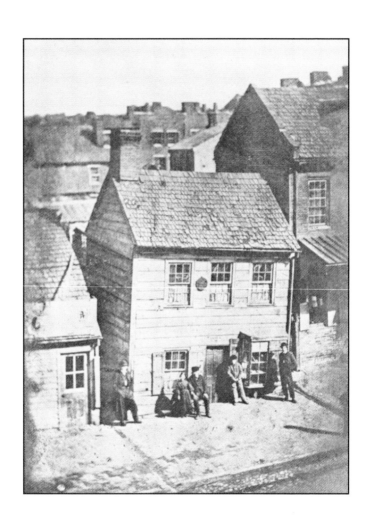

SULZEBACHER HOUSE

900 block West Baltimore Street

Mid-nineteenth-century photos of this battered but proud old house appear in a few Baltimore publications when the age of gravure arrived, proving that when it was destroyed (probably about 1880) it was regarded as a specimen of quaint old days.

Built: probably mid-eighteenth century. Razed: date unknown.

THE ADAM BOSS HOUSE

South Bond Street

T his ancient old clapboard cottage was believed to have been refurbished in 1782 for Revolutionary soldier Adam Boss. The family included three veterans of the 1812–1814 war, one of whom didn't leave the premises until 1887. This may have been the oldest structure, period, in Baltimore history.

Built: about 1710. Razed: date unknown.

THE OLD CARPET LOOM
BUILDING

Northwest corner of Redwood and Liberty Streets

Visitors in search of the "picturesque" during the romantic 1890s were not allowed to miss the old "carpet loom" building, perhaps one of the birthplaces of Baltimore industry, but by the time this photograph was made, home of Thomas Burke and his no doubt well-patronized saloon.

Built: 1740s? Razed: date unknown.

THE OLD CURIOSITY SHOP

West Saratoga and North Eutaw Streets

J udging from the specimens in his windows, R.A. Reed, the shopholder, dealt mainly in prints and books, but this picture is proof that even 100 years ago (the photograph appears to have been taken about 1870-80) the collecting craze was ready to blossom on home turf.

Built: probably about 1770-80. Razed: date unknown.

FIRST CITY POST OFFICE

On Front Street, near Exeter

This glorified shed, with its solid shutters and a heavy door for security, served as the city's first post office, really a mail drop for Annapolis- and Philadelphia-bound couriers. Mary Goddard, the city's first postmistress, moved the office downtown to Baltimore and South Streets in 1775 and it is her second post office–printing business that figures in the exciting Revolutionary years. Built: 1751. Razed: date unknown.

KAMINSKY'S TAVERN

Grant and Mercer Streets

This engaging old warren of urban vernacular architecture may have been Baltimore's first public building. Its ancient origin is evident from the gambrel roof. Its survival for 118 years was surprising since the location was central and the place outmoded by more fashionable resorts like the Indian Queen and the Fountain Inn when it was a mere half-century old.

Built: about 1752. Razed: 1870.

FIRST CITY-COUNTY COURTHOUSE

The bed of Calvert Street between Fayette and Lexington

E arly renderings of this structure, certainly one of the more bizarre moments in Colonial vernacular, show a courthouse on stilts, since in 1785 the city fathers ran Calvert Street *under* the court building, leaving it standing on a pair of berms; a remarkable, if somewhat shaky economy.

Built: about 1768-70. Razed: about 1810.

CONGRESS HALL

Hopkins Place and Lombard Street

S trictly speaking, this was Baltimore's most historic building, based on the outcome of decisions made there. Though little more than an overblown house, Philadelphia-style, the straightforward building, believed to have been built by one Henry Fite as an inn, is where a panicky Continental Congress granted dictatorial powers to Washington in the winter of 1776-77.

Built: 1760s. Burned: 1860.

FOUNTAIN INN

East side of Light Street between Baltimore and Redwood

George Washington slept here and apparently drank here also, judging from the incredible bar tabs run up at civic receptions in his honor. The spot is notable in that it has been serving as a transient facility for about 200 years. After the Fountain was torn down, the Carrollton Hotel took its place. Then, after the Carrollton burned, the Southern Hotel blossomed on the spot. The hotel closed a few years back and the building may be doomed.

Built: about 1773. Razed: date unknown.

THE GENERAL WAYNE INN

West Baltimore and Paca Streets

Not a coaching inn with an interior courtyard, like some of the more pretentious places farther downtown, the General Wayne preserved for an incredible length of time the tone of the Revolutionary generation architecturally. From tavern to top floor cut-rate dormitory, it was a tribute to Baltimore's first great expansion period and the west side grain trade. A loft for the needle trades replaced it.

Built: 1785. Razed: 1892.

The Federal Period

The Baltimore of the Federal years is the first one that survived significantly into the age of photography. This was fortunate, since the appeal of the city's first important buildings is particularly adapted to being photographed. There is a fine, ordered cleanness, a sort of dressy clarity about the Federal structures, a *contrast* that does not emerge in the delicate renderings of the period, with their classic lines, but which in black and white reality jumps out unmistakably.

The period is notable, as architectural historians have noted long since, for the appearance on the scene of a quartet of designers, Latrobe, Godefroy, Mills and the senior Long, who coupled professional training with a glowing artistic talent. They are responsible for producing Baltimore's early Londonesque dash, its gloss of classic elegance. Much of this survived well into the Gilded Age of post-Civil War America, only to be demolished, largely within the decade of the 1880s, with the development of the government center at the turn of the century, an ambitious, if hardly premeditated plan. Virtually all of Federal Baltimore, from the Gay Street corridor all the way to the hill of St. Paul and Fayette far to the west, was to vanish under millions of tons of Beaux Arts architecture.

It was perhaps the least vicious, certainly the least sordid, of the city's conscious efforts to wipe out its past and keep "up to date." The men who consolidated the great court block between Calvert and St. Paul, who financed the soaring, airy lost Post Office and cleared the way for City Hall Plaza, were not mean-spirited and were honestly of the opinion that their replacements were honorable equals of the Federal masterpieces, as well as being vastly improved conveniences for the public.

The Federal era was not only distinguished for its architects, but also for a sudden jelling in land values. We hear of $5,000 being paid for urban lots used for the erection of mere houses as early as 1817, sure evidence that Baltimore was becoming a very desirable town base. All of this happened, beginning in the 1790s, with a relatively sudden rush. By 1800 the city had not supplied itself with such occasional public elegances as New York had achieved in the Tontine Coffee House or St. Paul's Chapel Broadway or Federal Hall. Only a few blocks had begun to take on the elegance of Philadelphia's Walnut Street, with its four-story townhouses, basement street entrances for merchants' goods, brick solidity and nice Georgian detailing.

By 1820, however, Baltimore had made the artistic and social transition. The great Latrobe Exchange, with its domed grandeur, was in place, and so was Milleman's elegant new Courthouse and Long's exquisite Union Bank. A new urban style was evolving, though perhaps more than nudged by the innovations of Robert Adam and other English classicists, and by no means confined to Baltimore.

30

The vanished "Montebello" of Baltimore's 1790s was like Antiquarian House in Plymouth, Massachusetts (1809) or Philadelphia's "Lemon Hill," both surviving specimens. Latrobe's Burd Mansion of 1801 in Philadelphia exhibited much of the Baltimore style—flat, lateral surfaces, plain windows in recessed arches, minimal and crisp eave lines, and a general Regency air of stateliness, sometimes faintly pompous. Robert Mills had used the recessed portico with two columns flush against two wings in the Sansom Street Baptist Church in Philadelphia, a design scheme suggestive of both "Tusculum," the Delphian Club of the Federal period, and the old Federal Courthouse, both in downtown Baltimore until the post-Civil War period.

Whoever gave the world Baltimore's first rural mansions their designs (there is almost no published documentation), they certainly had a singularly unfortunate survival rate. This is indicated in a quite interesting and documentary way in the Findlay chairs of 1805, now in the collections of the Baltimore Museum of Art. Little architectural vignettes of 17 country estates of the Federal period were sketched on these painted pieces of furniture. Only two of the estates, some quite elaborate, survived 150 years later (Mount Clare and Homewood).

Two parallel trends emerged in domestic architecture. One was to make the urban townhouse a thing of practical elegance, suitable for winter residence and heating. Another was to make country estates livable in Baltimore's soggy, mid-year months. The first requirement of the "quality," freeze-proof winter quarters, was provided in the form of projects like Waterloo Row and inventions like the Latrobe stove. The second trend saw the sprouting grandeur of porches, delightful decorative accents to such early summer resorts as "Willowbrook," "Montebello" and "Harlem."

Baltimore's Federal style is an important national quality—a moving one. For the first time the city felt its maturity by simply becoming cosmopolitan. One can feel the *rightness* of its style in the photographic survival.

THE GERMAN REFORMED CHURCH

Redwood Street between South and Gay

This church was called "Old Second" because it was the second home of a parish that occupied a simpler church at Baltimore and Front Streets until 1795. The slender spire, of exceptional quality, housed a town landmark. Also called the "town clock" church.

Built: 1796. Razed: 1866.

FURLEY HALL

East side of Brehms Lane at Herring Run

This was one of Baltimore's most graceful and harmonious late Georgian facades. The "Son of Liberty" Daniel Bowly (1745-1807) was an early owner of the once huge estate which figured in the Baltimore siege of 1814. By 1900 it had shrunk considerably but was still a perfect example of a secluded Maryland Colonial mansion with many outbuildings. The main home burned in 1906 and the remaining 26 acres were bulldozed in 1953 for a housing development.

Built: about 1778. Burned: 1906.

FIRST PRESBYTERIAN CHURCH

East Fayette Street and Guilford Avenue

Seating 1,000 persons and costing $20,000, the First Presbyterian was probably the most ambitious Maryland building of its decade. Martin Van Buren was nominated for President here in 1836. Mayor James Calhoun and General Samuel Smith were parishioners.

Built: 1789-95. Razed: 1860. Architects: Mosher & Dalrymple.

BELVIDERE

Calvert Street near Chase

Central Baltimore's most famous estate, today and even when it was thriving, was this handsome Colonial mansion to which Lt. Col. John Eager Howard, hero of the battle of Cowpens, could retire to nurse his Revolutionary memories. It faced northwest with the eastern wing of the house in the bed of what is now Calvert Street near Chase. Belvidere breakfasts were famous and guests included Lafayette. John S. McKim owned the mansion during the Civil War period.

Built: 1787-94. Razed: 1875.

LIGHT STREET METHODIST
CHURCH
(Lovely Lane)

Southwest corner of Light Street and Wine Alley

This meeting house of spacious simplicity replaced two previous Lovely Lane meeting houses, the founding churches of American Methodism. It was opposite the fleshpots of the Fountain Inn. Southern and Union factions of the Methodist conference split into two separate entities in this building during the opening months of the Civil War.

Built: about 1796. Razed: about 1872. Architects: G. & J. Wall.

FIRST CHRIST EPISCOPAL CHURCH

Northwest corner of East Baltimore and Front Streets

T his church, originally the home of the First German Reformed congregation, was completed in 1797 by Christ Church parish, which moved to Fayette and Gay Streets after a generation when the Front Street neighborhood became less saintly. Old Christ Church was inhabited by St. Andrews Episcopal Church in the 1830s. Stylistically, this church showed the evolution of the simple, early meeting house into a more pretentious, spired landmark.

Built: 1790s. Razed: date unknown.

THE WARNER HOUSE

615 Washington Boulevard, Ridgely's Delight

One of the city's last eighteenth-century tragedies was acted out on this lot when one of the last remaining early Federal survivals in the city was pushed over for a gas station. The finely-detailed old building was believed to have been the home of George Warner, a Fayette Street attorney in the times of Washington and Adams. A decade after the loss, Ridgely's Delight had become a fashionable renewal area, with homes reaching into the $60,000 to $90,000 class.

Built: about 1795. Razed: 1970.

HOLLIDAY STREET THEATER

East side of Holliday Street between Fayette and Lexington

Excited crowds watched the Ft. McHenry bombardment from the roof of this hoary shrine of the American drama. Despite its Coney Island drapery, the Holliday Street theater retained its graceful Regency outlines until the end. After an 1873 fire, the theater was rebuilt along the original lines. Adelina Patti, Fanny Kemble and Edwin Forrest starred here.

Built: 1794 (and rebuilt in 1813 and 1874). Razed: 1917.

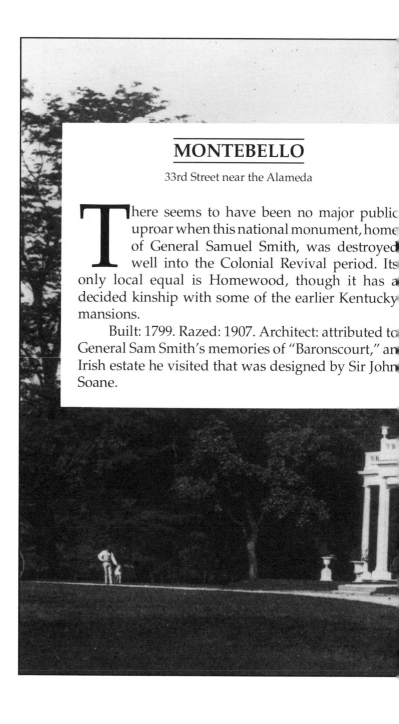

MONTEBELLO

33rd Street near the Alameda

There seems to have been no major public uproar when this national monument, home of General Samuel Smith, was destroyed well into the Colonial Revival period. Its only local equal is Homewood, though it has a decided kinship with some of the earlier Kentucky mansions.

Built: 1799. Razed: 1907. Architect: attributed to General Sam Smith's memories of "Baronscourt," an Irish estate he visited that was designed by Sir John Soane.

BOLTON

Hoffman Street at Bolton, Mount Royal

Of all Baltimoreans who aspired to a seat of princely elegance, none perhaps came as close as George Grundy of Bolton or his successor owner, William Wallace Spence. This lovely facade, perhaps the finest in the residential history of Baltimore, was torn down to build the Fifth Regiment Armory hall, put up to stimulate mid-town railroad station traffic and bring in delegates for the 1912 Democratic National Convention and the nomination of Woodrow Wilson for President.

Built: about 1800. Razed: early twentieth century.

THE OLD ASSEMBLY ROOMS

East side of Holliday Street between Fayette and Lexington

A stately affair of quite large scale that somehow suggested the White House, the Old Assembly Rooms were a privately sponsored venture underwritten in part by John Eager Howard. The building originally possessed a balustrade and central pediment that vanished when a third floor was added. By 1868, Baltimore City College was in residence but was burned out of its makeshift home by the Holliday Street Theater fire.

Built: about 1800. Burned: 1873. Architect: Robert Cary Long, Sr.

CLOUDCAPPED

Frederick Road at North Bend Road

One of the last of the Italianate mansions to succumb, Cloudcapped sat 450 feet above tidewater and is said to have been an observation post for the British fleet invasion in 1814. It was the summer retreat of the Taylor and Randall families. Federal authorities took over the property as a national cemetery in 1937, and wrecked the mansion later to make room for more graves.

Built: 1800, with additions later. Razed: about 1938.

THE UNION BANK BUILDING

East Fayette Street at Charles

Regarded as hopelessly frumpy by the time of the Grant administration, the Union Bank was a peerless masterpiece of restrained Federal styling in the middle of great local rivals, including the second courthouse building and the Old Assembly Rooms. It figured in the famous National Bank war between President Jackson and Nicholas Biddle.

Built: 1807. Razed: 1869. Architect: Robert Cary Long.

ST. PATRICK'S ROMAN CATHOLIC CHURCH

Northeast corner of Broadway and Bank Street

There is enough of a hint of Benjamin Latrobe in this monumental little church to make one wonder if the architect didn't run it up while at work on plans for his great Baltimore basilica. St. Patrick's was the most elaborate Catholic structure built locally up to its day and the parish, under a French Revolution refugee and priest, organized the city's first parochial school for boys. A rather ungainly Gothic Revival St. Patrick's replaced the first building in 1897.

Built: 1806-07. Razed: about 1896.

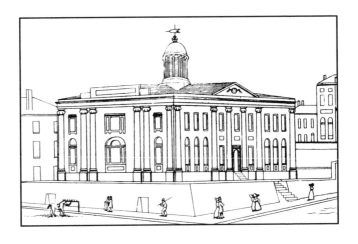

THE SECOND CITY-COUNTY COURTHOUSE

Southwest corner of Calvert and Lexington Streets

This building allowed Baltimore to shake off the laughable memory of its Revolutionary "courthouse on stilts" and to combine the various functions of city and county courts, title offices, the orphans' court and grand jury under one roof.

Built: 1806. Razed: 1895. Architect: G. Milleman.

OLD MASONIC HALL
(First Federal Court Building)

Northeast corner of St. Paul and Lexington Streets

A splendid facade, redolent of the more Napoleonic type of Federal architecture at its finest, the old Masonic Hall became a Federal courthouse in 1822. In this building Chief Justice Taney issued the opinion of *ex parte Merryman* in his famous confrontation with Abraham Lincoln over the writ of *habeas corpus*.

Built: 1814. Razed: 1895. Architect: Maximilien Godefroy (with, possibly, Robert Mills).

SLOAN-SINCLAIR MANSION

417 North Charles Street

A developer pushed over one of the last Federal remnants in the Mount Vernon district and the lot is now occupied by institutional offices. Upton Sinclair, muckraking novelist of the turn of the century, lived here in his youth. The top floors, including the eyebrow windows, are later additions to a townhouse that may have been by Robert Mills.

Built: 1812. Razed: 1969.

OLD LEXINGTON MARKET

Lexington and Eutaw Streets

Though this property was designated more than 200 years ago as a market site by John Eager Howard, apparently no market operated until about 1803 and no permanent structure was put up until just before the War of 1812. The old market added fish and was extended from Paca to Greene Street in the 1850s. In its heyday, during the 1920s, 1,100 stalls were in operation.

Built: originally about 1811, but many additions. Burned: several times, but devastatingly in 1949.

WATERLOO ROW

West side of the 600 block of Calvert Street

An elegant example of how to do an urban row in what was then countryside overlooking a swamp, Waterloo Row was said to have been a financial flop. But Mills' quietly broad homes, with their thick, beautifully proportioned millwork, set a new standard for their period. An archaeological remnant of this important vanished moment in American architecture can be seen in a Baltimore Museum of Art reconstruction.

Built: 1815-18. Razed: 1969. Architect: Robert Mills.

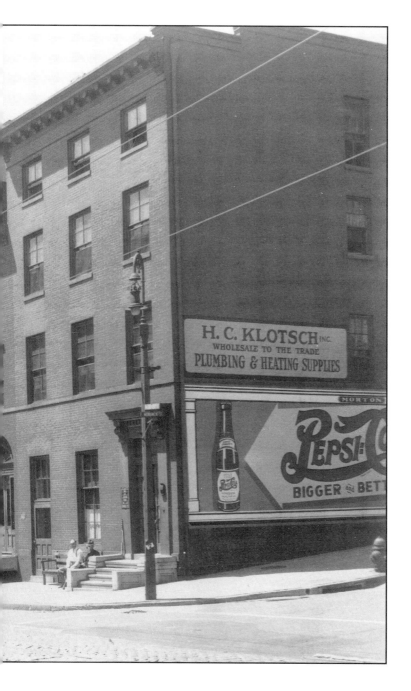

McNAMARA'S SALOON

227 North Calvert Street

This engaging little flophouse can serve as a stand-in for the many hundreds of vernacular saloons and corner spas that have disappeared from the central Baltimore scene in the past two generations, to be replaced by expensively trendy replicas of the "Gay Nineties." It is also notable for three reasons. It combines within itself three major architectural phases: eighteenth-century dormer, early Federal facade lines, and spiky Victorian gimcrackery at the street level. It also fuses the name of Baltimore's most famous defunct brand of beer, Gunther, with the real prototype, a genuine Irish pub. Its third more serious claim is the fact that it was the first permanent home (briefly in 1858) of the ancient Medical and Chirurgical Faculty of Maryland, the all-powerful state medical society.

Built: probably 1800-20. Razed: about 1905.

74

MARYLAND ACADEMY
OF SCIENCES

Northeast corner of Franklin and Cathedral Streets

Enoch Pratt gave this interesting little city mansion to the Maryland Academy of Sciences in 1891. George Hoffman was the original owner and it served as the Maryland Club from 1858 until 1891, except for a brief but exciting interval during the Civil War when it was commandeered by a Union Army general. The barrel-shaped portico was unique in the downtown area.

Built: about 1820. Razed: about 1906. Architect: attributed to Benjamin Latrobe.

76

ST. PAUL'S EPISCOPAL CHURCH

Charles and Saratoga Streets

The most lavish church of the Federal period, St. Paul's was found to be too "popish" by a Scottish traveler in 1818. It was actually the third home (on the same site) for St. Paul's and its Romanesque replacement has survived for a century and a quarter as a conspicuous ornament of the downtown district.

Built: 1816. Burned: 1854. Architect: Robert Cary Long.

78

HEBREW ORPHAN ASYLUM
(Calverton)

Frederick Road, 2.5 miles west of old city line

Built as the home of a banker, Dennis Smith, who went bankrupt, Calverton was converted almost at once into an almshouse and remained as a charitable home throughout its history. The original central block had a cupola, round third-story windows of Williamsburg type, and an amazing two-column, two-story portico with a catenary arch. Bays on the sides of the main facade completed this unique and in ways delightful structure, said to have been graced by a sculpture by Antonio Capellano who worked on the U.S. Capitol.

Built: about 1816. Burned: 1874. Architect: Joseph Jacques Ramée.

EAST PLEASANT STREET

Unit block

These neighbors of the larger Murdock mansion, nearby and also gone, were of decided Historic American Buildings Survey calibre before being pushed over for commercial development. With their blend of Bostonian elegance and wide-spirited Southern charm, they were perhaps the classic examples from many that dotted the court district up to the early twentieth century.

Built: about 1820. Razed: 1935.

FIRST BAPTIST CHURCH

South Sharp and Lombard Streets

Affluent Baptists paid $50,000 for this classic essay in Roman domemanship and it has always been an architectural lesson in how to achieve monumentality within small scale, for the building was not large. Possibly an early stimulus to the 1830-60 Gone-With-the-Wind portico orgy in the southeast and Gulf states.

Built: 1817. Razed: 1877. Architect: Robert Mills.

JONESTOWN

East Baltimore Street east of the Falls

This is an early view, possibly even predating the Civil War, of East Baltimore Street, looking east at High Street, in the heart of "Jonestown," as the district was titled in the eighteenth century, when the streets were known as York and Granby respectively. The 1904 fire halted just two blocks behind the photographer, but low-grade commercial uses battered these blocks to bits in the first half of the twentieth century and replacement buildings were mostly characterless.

Built: 1732-1820. Altered: 1910-70.

SOUTH CHARLES STREET

Corner of Lee Street

This solid row, whose dormers were unconsciously repeated in the Gail & Ax-Lorillard tobacco plant adjoining, was typical of the nineteenth-century vernacular architecture provided for average citizens. Charles Street, for reasons lost to history, detoured around this block, then took off in a straight line for four miles through the heart of the city.

Built: probably 1830s. Razed: early 1970s.

THE LORMAN ROBERTS HOUSE

Southeast corner of Charles and Lexington Streets

An elegantly-scaled little town mansion that somehow suggested Regency London, the Lorman Roberts House occupied the most central corner in what was for about a century headquarters for the Maryland real estate industry. The original owner came to Baltimore in 1790 and established himself in the clipper trade.

Built: probably about 1825. Razed: 1889. Architect: attributed to Robert Cary Long, Jr.

GUY'S MONUMENT HOUSE

East side of Court Square between
Fayette and Lexington Streets

William Guy's house was one of the landmarks of busy "Monument Square," as it was then known, and beautifully in scale with the Battle Monument shown. Its basement oyster bar was widely admired and Charles Dickens gave Guy's a bit of literary immortality when he proclaimed the house's specialty an "enchanted julep," a drink he shared with Washington Irving. After it had to move for the Old Post Office project, Guy's moved into the Gilmor House (St. Clair Hotel) and kept the old name alive for a few years, until dispossessed by the court project. From a stereo by William M. Chase.

Built: about 1820. Razed: about 1888.

THE LATROBE BLOCK

The 400 block of Cathedral Street

This stately block, shown from the steps of Latrobe's Basilica of the Assumption, was an elegant cul-de-sac housing the fortune of the city from the late Federal period onward. Its site now houses the Pratt Library's central branch. B. H. Latrobe designed one of the row's mansions for Robert Goodloe Harper.

Built: 1845. Razed: about 1930.

THE BALTIMORE EXCHANGE AND CUSTOM HOUSE

Gay and Water Streets

Latrobe, with help from Maximilien Godefroy, produced this unique Graeco-Roman design with an airy dome that had catwalk promenades from which ladies could be shown the inner harbor basin and its shipping. Lafayette was received here and Abraham Lincoln lay in state under the dome.

Built: 1819. Razed: 1901-02. Architect: Benjamin Latrobe.

TUSCULUM
(The Delphian Club)

On Bank Lane near St. Paul Street

A grove of trees all but covered this little Greek essay, quixotically almost in the heart of town behind the bustle of Barnum's City Hotel. The home of William Gwynn, it was also headquarters for the Delphian Club, 1820s literary and legal lights who were joined from time to time by bigger fish, including Jared Sparks, John Howard Payne, J.P. Kennedy, and Rufus Dawes.

Built: about 1820. Razed: 1891. Architect: Robert Cary Long. Portico by Robert Mills.

THE WESTERN POLICE STATION

Greene Street between West Fayette and West Baltimore

This canopied little municipal way station, complete with bell tower, had one of the nation's first remote alarm systems. The canopy of canvas was standard in its period on all public and commercial structures. It was replaced in 1878 by a Victorian extravaganza further west on Pine Street between Saratoga and Lexington. Built: about 1825. Razed: 1922.

The Antebellum Years

Quite suddenly, about the year 1830, Baltimore architecture seems to diversify. What had been a more or less unified Federal tradition, insisting on a relative modesty in domestic housing and public building and banded to a quite restrained classicism, lurches suddenly into the eclectic.

Perhaps we should not be surprised by such an abrupt change, for it is clear that the Colonial village of 4,000 to 5,000 souls was being rapidly buried under new construction. When Robert Gilmor, Jr., presenting a paper to the Maryland Historical Society in the 1840s, speaks of the Baltimore of his youth in the Revolutionary and early Federal periods, it is almost as if he is describing a lost civilization.

With the early Victorian age we can, perhaps, feel a much closer kinship, if only because its forms in furniture and graphic arts have been through a fashionable recent revival. Architectural critics and aestheticians used to describe this obvious rift in American design with horror, as a sort of sudden relapse into almost criminally frivolous drapery, but we do not quite see things that way today. For one thing, the Gothic Revival interiors that we once scorned so roundly seem today, in many cases, to be more adaptable to our modern interest in overhead lighting and central heating than the vast Greek Revival barns that so many people favored in the early nineteenth century.

The pre-Civil War years were, however, preeminently *not* the years of the Gothic house, though this was a lively subspecies of domestic building, but rather the years of Gothic institutions: churches, parish houses, schools and colleges. The dominant format in the early Gothic church revival in America seems to have been made up of relatively simple samples of perpendicular styling with towers suggestive of Somersetshire England—flat-topped affairs standing in the center of a gable end with sprockets and machicolated brackets around the eave line. Baltimore, however, loved its soaring tapered spires and cupolas. Richard Upjohn had introduced huge broached spires, typical of the English midlands, into his Northeastern masterpieces of church design. John Notman of Philadelphia also perfected this more pointedly spiritual style, and built at least one specimen of masterly grandeur, Emmanuel Episcopal Church, Cumberland, on Maryland soil.

It is a sad thing to observe that most of our Gothic specimens of antebellum date, including the finest houses and the two best institutional specimens, old Odd Fellows Hall and the second City College building, have vanished long since.

Not much better is the record of survival for another category of building from this period—the Italianate. These vast "mansion houses," with their towers, arched doorways and thick moldings, were built on literally every azimuth of the Baltimore suburban countryside. Some were of national importance. "Alexandroffsky's" great semicircular garden front was a theme repeated in a Hanseatic framework in the Lockwood-Mathews Mansion (1868), still standing in Norwalk, Connecticut.

While the Gothic or cottage Gothic style was far more suited to the vagaries of late Empire and early Victorian furniture than heavy Greek Revival rooms with their stiff, Pullman car effects, or darkly drafty Italianate mansions, it was the classic style that had the most appeal and attention in Baltimore architecture.

The Baltimore Greek Revival townhouse has relatively few prototypes elsewhere during the period of its glory, generally from about 1830 until the Civil War. Oddly, the Baltimore type seems to have been more prevalent in similar centers (in point of age) like Cincinnati and St. Louis than in sister cities on the East Coast.

The Baltimore type was at once generously wide enough to have a marked difference from the homes of comparable size in New York City, and bolder and coarser in detail than similar specimens in Boston. It was not exactly the style either for Jacksonian Washington, though the stately Slidell Mansion, built in 1845 on Lafayette Square but razed in 1922, would have felt perfectly at home in Baltimore's Mount Vernon district, with its classic version of the Baltimore double-columned entrance portico.

Richmond and Washington usually had more room and more flat areas for freestanding homes at or near the central business districts in the pre-Civil War years, although

Baltimore's Abell and Johns Hopkins Mansions and a few other downtown mansions had generous lots. The more common Richmond-Washington urban mansion was typified by the shuttered Wylie House, which vanished on Thomas Circle, Washington, in 1947, or the big single-family homes that used to decorate Richmond's West Franklin Street district and still survive in the Church Hill restoration. In Washington's case, even private homes were designed at least partially as transient housing, and many facades exhibit a sort of judicial heaviness, cumbersome fanlighting and window arching, plastered over domestic facades of some pretention. By contrast, in Baltimore delicacy remained the rule throughout the Federal period and well into the Victorian until the Italian boom of the 1850s. About the same time the tightly-done brownstone row house, almost wholly missing from Richmond and Washington, began decorating blocks north and west of Mount Vernon Place with its "chocolate sauce" effect.

While much of this building, though attractive, was a fairly mechanical use of a sort of classic vernacular, the city was not free of innovations of world moment or of architectural talent that could be exported. Until it was totally outclassed in 1867 by John McArthur, Jr.'s enormous Second Empire block for the Philadelphia *Public Ledger* building, the Sun Iron building in Baltimore was the most advanced and prepossessing structure in American publishing. Architectural discipline began to become formalized, and the city was fertile enough to start exporting its own architectural talent. R. Snowden Andrews (1830-1903) was a local architect and amazingly young when he did the magnificent, 30-room Riggs Mansion on Farragut Square, Washington, an Italian Revival masterpiece demolished in 1936.

An earlier tradition lived on in the Baltimore suburbs and the mill towns surrounding the city. Vernacular of the lower South was repeated by Baltimore County tradition in buildings like the surviving and restored Ballestone House at North Point, an inn-like double-piazza building with a thousand prototypes from Virginia to the Gulf and a virtual twin in Eufaula Tavern, built in Alabama in 1836.

Much of Federal Baltimore and virtually all of its early Victorian building remained in place until the 1890s, with one dramatic exception. The first mass-clearance activity that is well recorded in Baltimore history (a flood in the late 1860s helped to remodel the Jones Falls landscape) happened one midsummer day in 1873 when a spark from a boiler in the J. Thomas & Sons sash and blind mill apparently caught a shavings box on fire. The mill, at Park Avenue and Clay Street, was consumed in minutes, and fire brands started spreading the blaze in a strong breeze.

Explosions in a paint store, and the dry walls of old tenements along Clay Street, a virtual alley and an apparent "red light" district as well, helped feed the blaze, and by 12:30 P.M., two hours after it had started, the fire had generalized and spread into a four-block area. Desperate attempts to save the huge Central Presbyterian Church on the southwest corner of Saratoga and Liberty Streets failed and its spire went up like a torch. The fire ate through another distinguished structure from the rear, gutting the 47-year-old English Evangelical Lutheran Church on Lexington Street, between Park Avenue and Howard Street.

Volunteer firefighters mounted the roofs of the big mansions on Saratoga Street and to the north, wetting down St. Paul's Rectory and the homes of A. S. Abell and Johns Hopkins and fighting bucket brigade style, with some success. In the process of the conflagration, one Lizzie Miller, a Clay Street lady whose occupation can only be guessed, complained that she lost $3,000 in bank bills and $20,000 in diamonds. *The Sun* commented on this and other losses with the words that "hovels and houses of the worst repute" had gone up and that the district was now "all cleaned and purified by the almighty power of God."

All told, nearly four square blocks of the northwestern edge of downtown were lost to the fire. It created a wasteland that was hurriedly sketched on the scene and then rushed into the sensational New York graphic papers as the horror story of the week. Both the distinguished victims of the fire, the Central Presbyterian Church, built in 1855 for $70,000, but insured for only $18,000, and the Lutheran Church, insured for a mere $13,800, were lost to the neighborhood. Congregational elders voted to move out.

The great Clay Street Fire, however, left the old court district untouched, and it did nothing to halt the stupendous thud of huge row houses and elaborate churches, spawning for miles up the slopes of West Baltimore toward Rolling Road. It would remain for civic clearance projects, the 1904 fire, and sheer neglect, to finish off "old Baltimore" as the Civil War century knew it.

CENTRAL PRESBYTERIAN CHURCH

Southwest corner of Saratoga and Liberty Streets

An ornament just below the grandeurs of Mount Vernon, the Central Church was an eye-popper of the Tuscan manner if there ever was one. It was incinerated in the great Clay Street Fire of 1873, despite desperate efforts to save it and the handsome tower. The architect to date is obscure, but the hand of Niernsee and Neilson can probably be imagined in its flat, awkward, but honest planes.

Built: 1855. Burned: 1873.

OLD ODD FELLOWS HALL

Northeast corner of Gay and Lexington Streets

Т his was the mid-nineteenth-century home for the only national fraternal order founded in Baltimore. The Odd Fellows Hall, with the Lutherville Seminary and the old City College building, illustrates the appeal that Gothicism had for educational and institutional builders. It also shows that Robert Cary Long, Jr., had a fine adaptive hand in enlarging Caldwell's design. The Odd Fellows, no longer headquartered in Baltimore, went on to build themselves a Romanesque temple on the northwest corner of Saratoga and Cathedral Streets.

Built: 1831 with additions in 1843 and 1847. Razed: 1890. Architects: William Q. Caldwell with wings by Robert Cary Long, Jr.

THE JOHNS HOPKINS
TOWNHOUSE

18 West Saratoga Street

A quietly distinguished (and unusual freestanding) version of Greek Revival townhouse, Mr. Hopkins' home, bought in 1851 for $50,000, became a parking lot on the northern edge of what had been the pre-1800 town. The great philanthropist wrote his will here ($7 million in bequests) and died here in 1873.

Built: about 1830. Razed: 1933.

114

THE ATHENAEUM CLUB BUILDING

Northeast corner of Charles and Franklin Streets

A thousand homes of the gentry from Natchez to Nantucket used the four-column Ionic theme to add antebellum grandeur and this was one of the finer ones, notable in that unlike most Mount Vernon mansions, it was freestanding with a small garden. First a private home, the building then became one of the snootier downtown men's clubs. For 80 years the structure stood as a valued pendant, matching the equally elegant bulk of Godefroy's First Unitarian Church, at the gateway to the Mount Vernon district. The portico of the Athenaeum was salvaged and reerected at "Olney," a distinguished Harford County mansion.

Built: 1829. Razed: about 1910. Architect: William Small.

115

116

THE ENGLISH EVANGELICAL
LUTHERAN CHURCH

North side of Lexington Street between Howard Street and
Park Avenue

More than 500 weddings were performed before the Civil War in this fashionable downtown church, close to the raffish stables and fleshpots of Clay Street. The splendid Greek Revival false front was a later addition.

Built: 1826 and enlarged after 1832. Burned: 1873.

BARNUM'S CITY HOTEL

Southwest side of North Calvert Street at Fayette

David Barnum's City Hotel, by all odds the greatest hostelry historically in city history, is known to us first in delicate engravings of the Jacksonian period which show a restrained, Classic building on the order of Boston's elegant Tremont House. By the 1860s it had been gussied up like some aging dowager with bulging iron balconies. Dickens loved the place and John Wilkes Booth met Samuel Arnold here during the Civil War. The unsavory "Baltimore Plot" of 1861 menacing Abraham Lincoln was supposedly centered in Barnum's basement barber shop. The hotel was leveled to make room for the majestic Equitable building, a Romanesque marvel that still stands, and survived the fire of 1904 that wrecked the adjoining Baltimore and Ohio building.

Built: 1826. Razed: about 1889. Architect: William Small with alterations by Nathan Starkweather.

GLEN ELLEN

Loch Raven, Baltimore County

One of America's earliest Gothic homes, the Robert Gilmor country place fell apart in the 1920s mainly through civic apathy. Its model was "Abbotsford," Sir Walter Scott's estate in Scotland,
Built: 1833. Razed: 1929.

THE CHURCH OF THE MESSIAH

Gay and Fayette Streets

This distinguished Classic structure, notable for its Roman, coffered ceiling and its belltower, the city's first and finest, was the only religious victim of the Great Fire of 1904. Originally Christ Episcopal Church until that parish moved to stylish Mount Vernon in the 1870s, the Messiah's building was rebuilt in high Georgian, but the parish moved to suburban Hamilton in 1921, after 125 years of downtown worship. The later church became a movie just off Baltimore's downtown tenderloin strip.

Built: 1835. Burned: 1904.

UNITED STATES APPRAISERS STORES

Lombard and Gay Streets

This stupendous structure, with groined arches and vaulted ceilings throughout, cost the national government $241,000 in the Jacksonian era. Walls were three feet thick but the facade, though heavy, was one of arched grace. Oblivious to the inferno of 1904, the great warehouse awaited the death warrant of the Treasury Department for three decades. An Art Deco masterpiece, also appraisers stores, stands on the spot.

Built: 1839. Razed: 1933.

OLD RECORD OFFICE

Northwest corner of St. Paul and Lexington Streets

Although Architect Long supplied a more elegant Egyptian design originally, what got built was this heavy tomblike fireproof, regarded as the last word in record preservation for its day. The old fort stood as an ornament of the court district until the building of the new turn-of-the-century court structure. It housed both city and county records of its day.

Built: 1836-40. Razed: about 1895. Architect: Robert Cary Long, Jr.

EUTAW HOUSE

Eutaw and West Baltimore Streets

The great rival in its day of Barnum's City Hotel, the Eutaw had 125 feet of frontage on Eutaw Street. Robert Garrett & Sons bought the place in 1845 and owned it for many years, giving it first class management under Capt. Robert B. Coleman, the elegant master of New York's Astor House. General Lew Wallace, of *Ben Hur* fame, made the Eutaw a headquarters stopover for troops of the Union in the Civil War.

Built: 1835. Razed: 1912 and 1916 (in stages). Architect: Samuel Harris.

FRONT STREET THEATER

Front Street between East Baltimore and Plowman

B y the 1830s Baltimore had provided itself with a convention center and both Stephen Douglas and Abraham Lincoln were nominated for President in this 4,000-seat circus building. P. T. Barnum's monster show for Jenny Lind pulled a $60,000 box office in the place and the stage had nine-foot ways for the eye-popping on-stage arrival of horses and carriages.

Built: 1829 and rebuilt in 1838. Razed: 1904. Architect: William Minifie (of second theater).

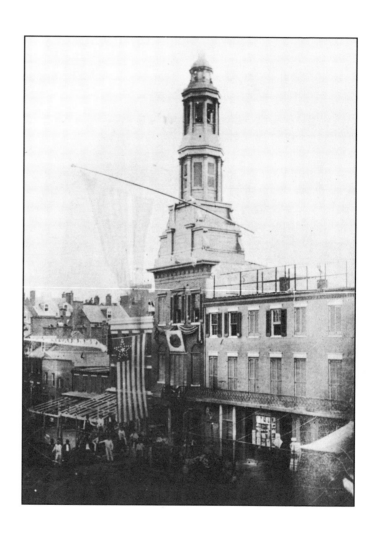

NEW MARKET FIRE HOUSE

Eutaw Street near Lexington

The boisterous and on occasion riotous New Market company occupied this building during the civic disturbances of the 1850s, battling rival companies sometimes to the point of fatalities. Its members must have been affluent (John Eager Howard founded the New Market) to have afforded the rather good early Georgian tower, even though it is rather incongruously linked to the firehouse base. The New Market, says fire department records, was retired from service in 1859. This photo may represent a permanent company in residence since it is believed to date from the Appomattox celebration in 1865.

Built: probably 1830s. Razed: date unknown.

THE MARYLAND
HISTORICAL SOCIETY
(The Baltimore Athenaeum)

Northwest corner of Saratoga and St. Paul Streets

This Florentine palace was built to house not only the historical group, then only four years old, but also the city library association and the Mercantile Library. After a brief whirl between 1918 and 1930 as the state's motor vehicle administration, it was demolished to make room for a parking building.

Built: 1848. Razed: 1930. Architect: Robert Cary Long, Jr.

THE MARYLAND STATE TOBACCO WAREHOUSE

Conway and South Charles Streets

A virtual twin of the magnificent, older appraisers stores building in the north harbor, this west side monolith could store up to 8,000 tons of hogshead tobacco in its day. One of the state's earliest and grandest public works, redone elaborately in the mid-1930s, the enormous classic loft was pushed over for an inner harbor lot with much effort but no public murmur.

Built: 1848. Razed: about 1970.

LEE HOUSE

908 Madison Avenue

Part of the then-stylish northwestern addition, this house was reportedly new when Robert E. Lee moved in in 1848 and stayed four years while Ft. Carroll was being built in the harbor. By the 1920s the home had become a combined rooming house and butcher shop. It is amusing and tragic at the same time that one of its owners, a store proprietor, complained about paying $2.50 a load for two loads of basement trash that had to be hauled away, including "old swords, pistols, officer's boots and other junk."(!)

Built: about 1846-47. Razed: 1957.

THE GILMOR HOUSE
(St. Clair Hotel)

West side of Court Square between
Fayette and Lexington Streets

The Gilmor House, with its spectacular wrought iron drapery, had a dashing reputation in its day and was a particular favorite for swank regimental troops of the city. Its kitchens served baked shad for the visit of Baron Renfrew (H.R.H. Prince Albert) but there is no record of a royal reaction to the Maryland specialty. (Also known as the St. Clair Hotel and, later, as Guy's Monument House.)

Built: about 1840. Razed: about 1897.

THE MARYLAND INSTITUTE

East Baltimore Street and Market Place

More than 350 feet long, Baltimore's grandest essay in the Italian style and perhaps the finest "market"-type assembly hall America ever possessed became a beautiful ruin in the 1904 fire and was not rebuilt. Both Presidents Pierce and Fillmore were nominated here. Lincoln spoke to a great "sanitary fair" gathering here on April 18, 1864.

Built: 1851. Burned: 1904. Architect: Reasin and Weatherall.

SUN IRON BUILDING

Southeast corner of Baltimore and South Streets

Perhaps the most innovative building ever planned by an American publisher, the Sun Iron building was the first of literally hundreds of arcaded lofts that helped make Baltimore one of the world's iron front valhallas. Astonishingly, it was planned and finished a year before the famous Crystal Palace, London, startled the world and ushered in modern architecture.

Built: 1850. Burned: 1904. Architects: Bogardus & Hatfield.

146

ALEXANDROFFSKY

Fremont Avenue and Hollins Street

There are few, if any, grander notes in the Italian revival than the semicircular conservatory and surmounting bay of this great urban mansion, built with Romanoff rubles and Winans millions made after Thomas Winans, railroading genius, had served the Czarist regime. An anchor of the old west side, when it went, so did vast reaches of an elegant old Victorian district.

Built: 1853. Razed: 1928.

WYMAN VILLA

Johns Hopkins University Campus, Homewood

Before its destruction by the university, Wyman Villa was the city's most distinctive Victorian house with all its furnishings intact. Richard Upjohn inspired the design for the home of William Wyman, whose family called it "Homewood Villa." When broken up in the mid-1950s, all it needed was about $50,000 in new plumbing and repairs.

Built: 1853. Razed: 1955.

CARROLL HALL

Southeast side of Baltimore Street at Calvert Street

This stately hall, in 1895 the temporary home of the *Baltimore News*, was another fine Italianate inspiration for downtown Baltimore like the Maryland Institute. It was, especially in the Civil War period, a center for military and political meetings and behind its heroically-scaled windows was a large assembly room.

Built: probably 1850s. Razed: about 1900.

CALVERT STREET STATION

Calvert and Bath Streets

A favorite theme of the dominant Baltimore architects of the mid-nineteenth century, twin towers, dominated this Italianate building, set at an unusual, catercornered angle to its street corner. The Prince of Wales (later Edward VII) received a tumultuous welcome here in 1860 and the station was a headquarters for Gettysburg battle hospital relief and rail shipments.

Built: 1840-50. Razed: 1948. Architects: Niernsee and Neilson.

IMMACULATE CONCEPTION
CHURCH

Mosher and Division Streets

Shamelessly destroyed in a deal between the church and the short-term needs of a hospital, the Immaculate Conception Church was the finest example of Tuscan Baroque in the city. But in 1973 it was simply another marooned ecclesiastical masterpiece, though impeccable inside and sweepingly moving without.

Built: 1857. Razed: 1973.

EVESHAM

Near Northern Parkway at Tunstall Road

J oseph Patterson, a wealthy iron merchant and brother of the famed Betsy (1786-1866), is credited with enlarging an original home on the Drumquehastle tract into this neo-Gothic fantasy, one of the more delightful of the Baltimore area, but lost to housing development. A spiral staircase in iron and blind shutters for symmetry were features of the manse, which passed to the Reverdy Johnson, Jr., family on Patterson's death. The harbor was viewable from the cupola. A portion of Evesham was saved and incorporated into a Gibson Island residence.

Built: early nineteenth century and enlarged in the 1850s. Razed: 1961. Architect: attributed to Edmund G. Lind.

RAVENHURST

Near Towson

Pre–Civil War "Ravenhurst" was a fanciful masterpiece of the Gothic horror school of architecture built in the northeast section of Baltimore County. Its most famous owner was Major General I. Ridgeway Trimble, C.S.A., a major aide to Robert E. Lee. Ravenhurst burned in 1985 after unsuccessful restoration attempts.

Built: 1840-50 (probably). Burned and razed: 1985. Architect: unknown.

THE MALTBY HOUSE

East Pratt Street near Light

B y the 1850s, the commercial pressures on the city demanded first-class housing nearer the docks than the Monument Square institutions and this was one of the answers. The Maltby, between the Camden Station hub on the west and docks just to the east, was a crossroads of commercial transients, especially Virginians and drummers of the southern trade. Its cuisine, however, was reported far from ordinary.

Built: 1855. Burned: 1904.

"GUILFORD."
RESIDENCE OF A. S. ABELL.
YORK ROAD, BALTIMORE CO., MD.

GUILFORD

200 block of Wendover Road

This great 52-room estate, home in the last half of the nineteenth century for the lordly Abell family of Baltimore *Sun* fame, was the largest private house in the state until it was demolished for development of a deluxe home community that bears its name.

Built: 1857-58. Razed: 1914. Architects: Lind & Murdoch.

GARRETT MANSION

Southwest corner of Monument and Cathedral Streets

This was one of the grandest of the antebellum townhouses and was inherited from her father, Robert Garrett, by Miss Mary Garrett, who left the property to the Carey family. A single sculpture by Gertrude Vanderbilt Whitney was all that adorned it in the modern art line when the Baltimore Museum of Art opened for business here in February 1923. When the museum acquired a handsome new home in Wyman Park at the end of the 1920s, the old mansion was demolished. It had included an amazing "East Indian Room," crafted in India to designs of Lockwood Deforest. An ordinary apartment house replaced the building, probably the outstanding loss to date in the Mount Vernon area, Waterloo Row excepted, though the Alexander Brown mansion a block north and Charles Street's Swann mansion were also notable.

Built: about 1860. Razed: about 1930. Architect: Louis Long (with gallery additions by McKim, Mead & White).

IRON FRONTS

Baltimore Street East and West

Iron fronts nudged their way into the main business artery, rubbing shoulders with grander masonry and brick, a scene incinerated in 1904. This is Baltimore Street looking west along the north side of the street, in a stereo by W.M. Chase made probably about 1875. The tall building in the center (with wall sign) was the Murphy Printing Company at No. 182 West. The building became 104 East in the renumbering of 1887.

Built: 1850-75. Burned: 1904.

CHARLES STREET

North from Saratoga

Not a single residential block of Charles Street in the midtown area has survived unaltered and this one has wholly vanished under commercial buildings, the earliest dating back into the 1870s. The 1878 photo gives a good idea of housing for the gentry during and after the Civil War.

Built: 1820-50. Razed: late nineteenth century.

SOUTH CHARLES STREET

From Pratt to Barre Streets

This ancient district, known as "Frenchtown" after early refugee-settlers from Acadia, was a large, mostly unaltered warren of late eighteenth- and nineteenth century buildings, with later iron fronts here and there, when wrecked by the Inner Harbor West plan. It was the last vestige of old wharf housing and merchant history in the immediate downtown.

Built: largely from 1790s to 1850s. Razed: 1965-70s.

The
High Victorian Triumph

A s with many other American cities of its vintage, Baltimore's greatest period of physical growth came in the late Victorian age. By 1890, the city had built more than 350 churches and 90,000 dwelling houses, or something like 40 percent of all the housing added since then.

The Baltimore of the white steps signature was really born in this age, and it created whole colonies of workers and craftsmen, whole shoals of subcontracting industries working in metal, plaster, wood, iron, ceramic and masonry, supplying not just the hundreds of spreading blocks of the robust postwar city but other centers that lacked a source of stone or a brick and ironworking capability.

We may justly regard this period as the golden age of domestic housing, for never again would the citizens be supplied with dwellings literally built for the ages. Late Victorian housing could be highly speculative, but it was not often merely expedient, and sites were used in a more sophisticated way than is commonly alleged.

The almost endless blocks east of Broadway and west of Fremont Avenue were economically, but not really racially segregated, for most of the black population lived in a series of countless little alley developments that were strewn through every one of at least a score or more middle class row house sections.

When these sections began to become economically integrated, with low-income white migrant workers and blacks occupying significant blocks housing the gentry, the suburban residential flight accelerated. Blight too often followed as absentee landlords or families with few, if any, resources took over near-mansions previously maintained by tax-free incomes and servants—an impossible task of maintenance. This common pattern was most damaging in its day and despite some renovation remains a problem for Victorian quality housing, which has survived in surprisingly large batches.

It is Victorian housing, rather than the public buildings of the period, that probably was more important architecturally, given the long view of what was achieved. Very high standards were the norm. The Baltimore "panel" brickwork, complex geometric walls with their sudden corbels and rhythmic fenestrations, marked the progression of a sure-footed architecture in Mount Vernon, the Broadway district, the great western squares, and in Bolton Hill and older sections of the Charles Village district.

Wrought iron was used as a well-scaled complement everywhere, and surviving blocks show that Baltimore's vernacular architects, with a few awkward exceptions, were skilled at massing new housing against old backdrops without jarring juxtapositions—a finesse that has largely escaped modern planners.

When one moves on to public or official architecture, the picture is less pleasing. There is something parochial and stiff about Baltimore building from 1865 until nearly the turn of the century. The last really fine classic structure, the Federal Courts, had gone up in the closing months of the great conflict. Then, suddenly, there is a poverty of style, of grace, despite the fact that Baltimore designers had been in the forefront of professional architectural advance, helping found the American Institute of Architects just before the war and establishing one of its early strong chapters in the 1870s.

Baltimore design, which had had an originality of spirit, suddenly becomes imitative and not always successful as merely copyist. John W. Garrett's Baltimore and Ohio headquarters building, for instance, resembled in its massing Alfred Mullet's great Boston Post Office, razed in 1933, or the Executive wing of the White House (saved from destruction urged by the White House in the 1950s), but it was in no way as pure a specimen of the Second Empire manner.

One looks at the parade of specimens with some dismay—the clumsy and hooded Ford's Theater, the heavy buildings put up by Johns Hopkins sponsors, Enoch Pratt's first forbidding, heavy-spirited home, or the boom-town mansards of the Carrollton Hotel—and immediately senses that these are buildings with nothing of Baltimore's elegance of scale or restraint of surface as Long and Mills had made known. The Academy of Music was a splendid large hall, with magnificent and versatile equipment for its day, but the stiff arabesques of its facade expressed none of its glowing interior and it was at once provincial and pompous, a summary of what twentieth-century architects were to decry in their famous priestly canons that came to fruition in the 1950s.

Much of this architecture, of course, did not pretend to be serious. When John Dos Passos, a onetime dweller in the Govans area, looked up at the fantastic hooded pile of the American Brewery and called it "circus architecture," he expressed some of the late Victorian heartbeat. Buildings were meant to be fun in a world that seemed to be broadening and clearing. The little Moorish arcades and band shells, the Indian domed beach houses, were part of a joy in living that was repeated across the city in more pretentious structures like country homes, carbarns, and gatehouses.

The great tower added to the Old State Normal School may have been a whimsical extravagance and may have helped condemn this wonderful old fancy to the dump trucks, but it expressed the free longing of Victorian hearts for a world that had a glowing horizon as well as a romantic amplitude.

Much of Victorian Baltimore has gone and much has survived in remarkably large restored islands like Mount Vernon and Bolton Hill. In more precarious condition, the sections of the west and east side centered on Fulton Avenue and Broadway offer preservationists the greatest remaining challenge—in a period when adaptive housing and effective government aid seems to be vanishing.

It is of some comfort that mammoth transit and road planning exploits seem to have lulled, perhaps for the balance of the century, and that what damage has been done will not be expanded. The road pattern, for one thing, has been pretty much completed east of Broadway and west of Fremont Avenue, sealing off the two great remaining Victorian reservoirs from permanent damage of a public works nature.

Victorian Baltimore, as it was known on the near east and near west sides, vanished in slum clearance activities that accelerated in the early 1950s and began to slow down about 1970. The major Victorian public buildings were largely victims of two things, the 1904 fire and recent institutional indifference.

The housing remainder, both closer in to the downtown and further out, is still a wonderful heritage, rivalled only in Brooklyn, north Philadelphia, parts of Boston, and the weirdly complete Victorian towns of central New York and parts of the Midwest.

THE FEDERAL COURTHOUSE

Northwest corner of Fayette Street and Guilford Avenue

President Buchanan selected the site for this handsome courts building on a cabinet visit in May 1859 and it was built during the Civil War. With the exception of the Exchange, it was probably the most ambitious structure in the city up to its time, but it vanished during a land assembly for the post office addition. From a stereo view by Richard Walzl.

Built: 1862-65. Razed: about 1907.

CONCORDIA HALL

Southwest corner of Eutaw and Redwood Streets

German musical and literary interests and Jewish cultural organizations made this music hall headquarters in the post-Civil War period and Dickens lectured here in 1868. A near-riot ensued when Lincoln conspirator John Surratt attempted to present a program here on his return from Rome after the war. This was Baltimore's performing arts center until the Academy of Music was built in the 1870s, largely through efforts of Israel Cohen, philanthropist.

Built: 1865-66. Burned: 1891. Architect: Cluss and Kammerhuber.

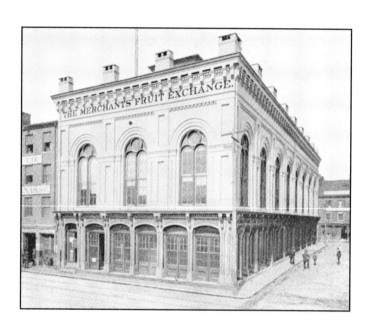

THE FRUIT EXCHANGE

Wood and South Streets fronting on Bowly's Wharf

When boat shipments dominated the trade, tri-weekly sales of Florida, California and local fruits were held here. The early Gothic windows were standard on market buildings of the day and were repeated at Broadway Market.

Built: about 1870. Burned: 1904. Architect: Niernsee and Neilson.

THE OLD RENNERT HOUSE

North side of Fayette Street between Calvert and Guilford

This was actually the second home for the Rennert. An early stereo view of the Battle Monument (see Guy's Monument House) shows a distinctly different Rennert House on the south side of Fayette. This building adjoined the Federal Courthouse and was razed for the post office project, after which the owner, flush with more than $200,000 in government cash, built the famous hostelry on the Liberty Street hill a few blocks west.

Built: 1871. Razed: 1881. Architect: George A. Frederick.

FORD'S OPERA HOUSE

Fayette and Eutaw Streets

Baltimore's greatest legitimate house was torn down to make a parking lot when it had rounded out nearly 100 years of theatrical history. Horace Greeley was nominated for President in the place, built by the fated John T. Ford of Washington for $175,000 and completely remodeled in 1893. A 2,200-seat ugly duckling, Ford's was still servicing road shows and tryouts into the mid-1960s, outlasting both its major competitors, Kernan's Maryland Theater and the Lyceum.

Built: 1871. Razed: 1964. Architect: James J. Gifford.

ST. JAMES HOTEL

Southwest corner of Centre and Charles Streets

This spiked and spired treasure of Goiter Gothic, developed by John Gittings, gave a Sherlock Holmes patina to the south end of the Mount Vernon Place development. It was sacrificed for a commonplace senior citizens' highrise that could have been built anywhere.

Built: 1874. Razed: early 1960s. Architect: Dixon and Carson.

THE OLD CLUBHOUSE

Pimlico Race Course, Pimlico Road

The lovely porches of "Crimea" mansion and the mansion house in Druid Hill Park are suggested in "Old Hilltop," the city's most tragic recent victim of fire. Steamboat Gothic with jigsaw it was, but no one who ever remembers it in its days of glory, and the food and drink served there, can forget that it preserved the nineteenth century in an especially gallant way, in the midst of the tawdry decay that surrounded the track in its later years.

Built: 1873. Burned: 1966.

THE ACADEMY OF MUSIC

West side of the 500 block of North Howard Street

This was Baltimore's social and theatrical center, with memories of Julia Marlowe, Modjeska, Adelina Patti, and Edwin Booth, until superseded in the theatrical arena by the Lyceum on North Charles and the Lyric Theater in the Mount Royal area. A portion of the old structure, though none of its interior or facade, remained in the walls of a modern movie house.

Built: 1874. Razed: about 1926. Architects: Niernsee and Neilson.

OLD STATE NORMAL SCHOOL

Northwest corner of Lafayette and Carrollton Avenues

The fountainhead of Maryland teacher education and almost 100 when consigned to the dump trucks by the educational establishment, Old State had a Hanseatic tower unequalled in the city for whimsy (unless by the surviving American Brewery building) and a general air of Ruskinian brio. It cost $100,000 in the hard coin of the era of plush.

Built: 1876. Razed: 1975. Architect: George F. Davis.

ST. MARY'S SEMINARY

Paca Street south of Druid Hill Avenue

S t. Mary's great Ruskinian Gothic block, the largest of its vein in the city, succumbed to the contraction of Catholic education in the city. Instead of the usual 1950s or 1960s parking lot, a neighborhood park—the lame and rather vacuous substitute in the 1970s for real renewal—occupies the site.

Built: 1878. Razed: 1975. Architect: E.F. Baldwin.

197

THE BALTIMORE AMERICAN
BUILDING

Southeast corner of Baltimore and South Streets

The powerful *Baltimore American* expected to put *The Sun* completely in the shade after putting up this towered masterpiece right across the street. The *American*'s debut set off a rivalry that raged for 29 years over who could drape the most bunting and gaslight flourishes on their building for community celebrations, parades, elections, and anniversaries.

Built: 1875. Burned: 1904. Architects: Dixon & Carson.

FAVA FRUIT BUILDING

West side of the 200 block of South Charles Street

Preservationists woke up late in the game to realize that the west harbor was almost gone and the city was persuaded to store this fine iron front facade, a prime specimen of the grandiose harbor plan's failure to blend old and new. The city convention center is on the site. The Fava facade was reborn in the 1980s as part of an inner harbor office project.

Built: 1869. Razed: 1976.

VICTORIAN INTERIORS, 1870-1900

Very few Victorian interiors, outside of a few churches and parish houses, have survived in the Baltimore area unaltered. Here are photos of what some were like. The library room, top, where prim young ladies no doubt got both tea and sympathy, is from the Academy of the Visitation at Park Avenue and Centre Street, a building scrapped 60 years ago for the Greyhound bus terminal. Below is the stair hall from Charles Bonaparte's country mansion, complete with orientals, a grandfather clock, bronzes and dark woodwork. Baltimore abounded in gentlemen's havens in the old days and the overleaf shows bearded scholars investigating a local library under the eye of a lady librarian. The setting is probably the Mercantile Library on Saratoga Street or a room in the pre–1904 Maryland Institute.

THE JOHNS HOPKINS
UNIVERSITY
DOWNTOWN CAMPUS

Little Ross Street between Eutaw and Howard

Though utilitarian to the point of ugliness, this was the birthplace of U.S. graduate studies, a cumbersome melange of sturdy, late-Victorian architecture almost hidden from view off busy Howard Street. The university escaped to the Homewood area after World War I.

Built: 1876 with additions through the 1880s. Razed: after 1920. Architect: Largely E.F. Baldwin.

208

HILLEN STREET STATION

Hillen Street at Exeter between High and Front

This spiky little downtown railroad station, whose design suggests the author of the Calvert Street Station of the 1850s, was John Mifflin Hood's proud signet that the Western Maryland Railroad he headed had arrived in the passenger business. Though it handled 42 trains a day in its prime, with connections for Frederick, Gettysburg, and the South Mountain country, the Hillen Street sputtered out in the early 1950s.

Built: 1876. Razed: 1955. Architects: Niernsee and Neilson.

A. HOEN & COMPANY

Lexington Street between Guilford Avenue
and Holliday Street

Designed to complement the north front of City Hall, the A. Hoen engraving factory housed the nation's oldest (established 1835) and finest printing plant for its day. A Sistine Chapel of Victorian graphics and advertising art, A. Hoen closed finally in 1981 after producing some of the most superb engravings ever issued on this side of the Atlantic.

Built: 1880. Razed: about 1926.

LIGHT STREET PIERS

The Chester River Steamboat Company, berthed here, was a major link to Eastern Shore tidal rivers. Inner harbor transit and commerce died in the 1940s.
Built: 1890s. Razed: about 1948-50.

THE OLD POST OFFICE

East side of Court Square between
Fayette and Lexington Streets

This exuberant specimen of World's Fair architecture became a victim of the agency it housed, the United States Post Office, when it was replaced on the same site by a boring classic building that blots out sunlight in this part of town. The main post office, needless to say, has since moved on to yet another building. Built: 1890. Razed: 1930.

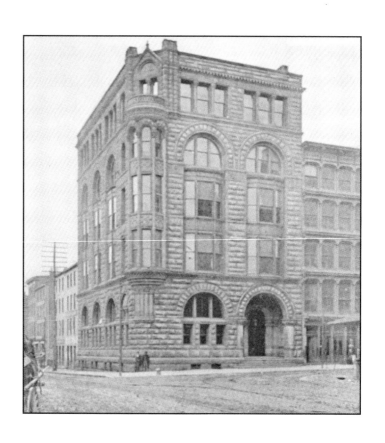

FARMERS' AND MERCHANTS' NATIONAL BANK

Lombard and South Streets

A small masterpiece of the Richardsonian Romanesque, the Farmers' and Merchants' was notable for its magnificent three-story corbelled corner bay and the splendid logic of its massing and fenestration. Possibly by Baldwin & Pennington and similar to their Fidelity Building, the banking center cost about $157,000 furnished, in 1890s money. Employees fled to a temporary office at the northeast corner of Charles and Saratoga after the 1904 blaze.

Built: 1888-89. Burned: 1904.

THE RENNERT HOTEL

The aura of this place continues to linger in the memory of elderly city gourmets. It always had distinction, especially in its dining room. Declining patronage in the 1930s left it with a $150,000 tax debt and it was destroyed, just when needed in World War II's transient housing debacle. A parking lot, one of the city's ugliest, replaced it.

Built: 1885 and enlarged in 1893. Razed: 1941. Architect: E.F. Baldwin.

THE ALTAMONT HOTEL

Eutaw Place and Lanvale Street

Hotelman-printer W.L. Stork sank his fortune into this extravagantly deluxe urban apartment hotel on expensive Eutaw Place where the land cost $400 a front foot. It had filtered water, a billiard room, and central heat, but also a very dumb 1960s custodian—the city's housing agency that tore it down.
Built: 1886. Razed: 1965.

THE LYCEUM THEATER

1200 block of North Charles Street

Edwin Booth and Lawrence Barrett opened this house commercially in 1890 in *The Merchant of Venice.* Previously, before application of the Romanesque stone drapery, it had been an amateur theatrical venture of the Wednesday Club. Swells of the 1890s watched the show from settees in the first ten rows of the orchestra.

Built: 1880s. Burned: 1925.

ENOCH PRATT FREE LIBRARY
(Old Central)

West Mulberry Street at Cathedral

Courthouse Romanesque was the style picked for the main branch of the Enoch Pratt Library, launched with 150,000 volumes and a $1 million endowment from its kindly namesake. The library itself razed this building in order to provide part of the lot for its huge central building opened during the 1930s on Cathedral Street.

Built: 1881-86. Razed: about 1930. Architect: Charles L. Carson.

226

THE MARBURG BUILDING

429 South Charles Street

One of the finest masonry lofts of its period in Baltimore, the Marburg building, like the Gail & Ax company's spectacular gabled tobacco factory nearby, heralded the city's once major role in the world tobacco market. The Marburgs were noted philanthropists. Eventually acquired by McCormick & Co., the handsome dark brick warehouse was razed in the same land deal that levelled McCormick's home office. With the passing of these structures, virtually the last relics of the city's inner harbor industry of the past (with the exception of the old power plant and the city sewage pumping station) have vanished.

Built: 1887. Razed: 1989. Architect: Charles L. Carson.

Maryland Theatre and Hotel Kernan,
Baltimore, Md.

THE MARYLAND THEATER

320 West Franklin Street

James L. Kernan, a Confederate veteran, developed this theatrical complex, complete with adjoining hotel, in the best Grand Hotel Negresco style. Despite a bad luck fire before it opened its doors, the Maryland became one of the nation's top vaudeville houses. Scott (Fitzgerald) and Zelda were patrons before it became a parking lot.

Built: 1903. Razed: 1951.

THE BALTIMORE & OHIO
HEADQUARTERS BUILDING

Northwest corner of Baltimore and
Calvert Streets (Cover)

The urban Second Empire style in somewhat corrupted, Moorish drapery, the Baltimore and Ohio Railroad building was nevertheless a wondrously elaborate symbol of Gilded Age plutocracy, with first floor walls five feet thick, built as the pride and joy of John W. Garrett, president of the road. The bricks from the burned-out hulk were reused in row housing on Patterson Park Avenue between Chase and Eager Streets.

Built: 1881-82. Burned: 1904. Architect: E.F. Baldwin.

BRYN MAWR SCHOOL

Cathedral and Preston Streets

Wealthy Miss Mary Garrett founded this distinguished young ladies' prep school almost single-handedly, with the help of an all-girl intellectual circle. The Romanesque Revival building was far larger than it looked and included a glistening tiled swimming pool. After Bryn Mawr moved to a suburban campus, the building lived on as the Deutsches Haus, a social and musical center for German-Americans of the city. Joseph Meyerhoff, real estate and insurance magnate, razed the building in order to make room for Maryland's new symphony hall, which he sponsored.

Built: 1888. Razed: 1973. Architects: Hornblower & Marshall.

CORNERSTONE BAPTIST CHURCH
(Har Sinai Temple)

Wilson and Bolton Streets

One of the most distinguished small religious buildings in the city, the Har Sinai Temple (later the Cornerstone Baptist Church) blended monumental stonework with an interior of superbly detailed neo-classic beauty. From the historic viewpoint it was doubly famous, as the home of the Har Sinai Congregation, at 150 the nation's oldest Reform group, and (in the 1960s) as a major center for the battle against segregation conducted by Maryland black activists.

Built: 1895. Burned: 1969. Architect unknown.

HOPKINS PLACE
AT LIBERTY STREET

This busy crossroads, with its little Roman tempietto (the National Exchange Bank) looking cosily important at the center, was a busy and balanced thing that helped define the character of west side Baltimore's business district. But by the 1930s parking and burgers by the bag had begun to encroach on its grandeur, as the photo shows.

Built: 1875-1920. Razed: (partially) late 1950s.

The Golden City Years

I

f social change doomed mid-Victorian buildings by the tens of thousands in the twentieth century, then the main damage to turn-of-the-century buildings, to our heritage of the Beaux Arts building, has been done by road builders, civic planners, and the city itself in league with private developers. The buildings of the Golden City period, that time when the grandiose urban plan that blossomed in the Chicago exposition of 1893 became a reality in dozens of American cities, generally from the 90s through the early 1920s, were by far the most lavish and the best engineered in American history. They can never be recaptured. They are *our* Versailles in that they are something that the nation and state will never again be able to *afford* to build—the Tiffany domes, mosaic ceilings, magnificent articulated masonry, bronze grilles and lampposts, the whole panoply of Edwardian living.

Only two of the structural victims shown or mentioned on these pages of turn-of-the-century landmarks actually burned down, and only two represent land being recycled by presumably helpless bankers maximizing profits. Of the balance, only four or five were done in by private owners who just didn't care or who preferred to recycle the land. Hundreds more can be ascribed to one form or another of urban obtuseness, often coupled with one-dimensional, linear planning activity—the American architect's and engineer's amazing inability to design harmonious buildings that fit into different time frames. Because the most recent decades have seen a flowering of adaptive use, an impression exists that our urban techniques have been refined and reformed—that we have sharply halted the rate at which destructive redevelopment vandalizes our heritage. Such is hardly the case. The majority of these structures have been demolished since World War II and most of them since the mid-1960s when the historic landmark program got going as an activist idea.

The first victims of renewal in the postwar period along the west side came with the "Civic Center" project of the 1950s, land clearance for a quite ordinary coliseum affair that is much too large and heavy for its lot and has been plagued from its beginning with structural faults. Hopkins Place had a certain sweep to it, a cosmopolitanism that reminded one of the crosstown squares of Manhattan as Broadway does its great diagonal through that city. It was a similar, wholly urban environment in the best sense, lively and the hub of city wholesaling. Here was the Brewer's Exchange building (still surviving and pleasingly restored), and (gone) the old Ganzorn restaurant, burned out of East Baltimore Street in 1904 but relocated at No. 11, where it lasted it out only long enough for the Eighteenth Amendment and Prohibition.

Architects of the turn-of-the-century period made an honest effort to give places like the Hopkins Place crossing some design unity and this is apparent in the astonishing "flatiron" effect of the National Exchange Bank, sitting on its island, surrounded by Graeco-Roman lofts, nicely scaled to the whole steamy, hospitable square.

The fact is that Baltimore architects had simply become more accomplished. E.F. Baldwin, who had done the ungainly, if fascinating, Baltimore and Ohio building in 1880, rose to mastery and elegance with later partners on such lost works as the Rennert Hotel and the old Sun building at Baltimore and Charles Streets. (The Baldwin and Pennington Maryland Court of Appeals building in Annapolis, senselessly destroyed by the state in order to create a Christmas card Colonial mall, was perhaps the finest ceremonial interior that ever blessed the state.)

Astonishingly little damage resulted to late Victorian building in the city from the legendary "Great Fire of 1904," if only because most of the buildings in its path dated from an earlier day. The foundation of the rising Custom House was weakened and had to be strengthened, and a few early skyscrapers (some still standing) were gutted.

The real damage to turn-of-the-century Baltimore was not done by its turn-of-the-century fire, but by the orgy of demolition that began in the late 1950s and continued without letup for two decades, until every vestige of the old waterside rim, everything (with the exception of a single church, an abandoned power plant, and one factory) was scraped away south of Lombard Street and east of Howard Street. None of the "Golden City" focal points were respected, if one excludes the rather sterile City Hall Plaza development and the southern end of St. Paul Place and

Preston Gardens.

In the 1970s, some effort to preserve what was left of the great early 1900s work was started, but far more specimens were demolished than remain. The 1904 fire took 1,545 buildings over about 140 acres of land, closely compacted in the north part of the inner harbor. Land condemnations alone rose to more than 400 in the far smaller (19 acres) clearance for Charles Center, and when it lurched into the harbor proper and sprawled over about 600 acres of land in three directions, the planners and developers clearly outmatched anything the forces of nature have accomplished before or since.

The Baltimore of the iron fronts is no more and neither is the Baltimore of the iron grilles and gates, the beautifully-elaborated buildings put up in that dim, tax-free past of the derby hat, steam beer, the corset and the carriage, what Van Wyck Brooks, the great American literary historian, called "The Confident Years."

Dr. Basil L. Gildersleeve, the great Greek scholar imported from South Carolina when Daniel Coit Gilman created the Johns Hopkins University, also characterized the age, and the city's role in it, when he said that Baltimore was a city of "high living and plain thinking."

Citizens were not, in other words, plain livers and high thinkers, that fibre of indestructible New England probity that had preserved itself for 250 years even when Gildersleeve said it. Baltimore had lived its life in a certain cocoon of gaiety and carelessness, and if there was grand permanence in the works of Latrobe and Mills, the real

Baltimore kernel, its essence, was in something else, the thought perhaps that we should build not for pretension but for simple living.

Perhaps this is why so much of our sheer housing has survived, while the great public structures on these pages are gone—because local people had an early and lasting confidence in the everyday, the practical, the personal and not the proud . . . . What is left us, scarred though it may be and even incomplete, stretches off, block by block . . . endlessly into the past.

244

THE SAFE DEPOSIT & TRUST COMPANY BUILDING

200 South Street

Razed for a commercial highrise, the old Safe Deposit & Trust Company was one of the very few survivals of the 1904 fire. There is some mystery about its original design, as a cornice date and the massive stodginess of the structure indicated an origin in 1876, but it was a unique survival in the old financial district, a sort of Graeco-Moorish tribute to the clutter and fun of the Victorian age. As a token gesture to preservation interests, the developer-owner of the lot incorporated part of the facade into his building plans.

Built: 1903. Razed: 1985. Architects: Baldwin & Pennington (1903) and Lawrence Hall Fowler (1929).

246

EMERSON HOTEL

Northwest corner of Calvert and Baltimore Streets

Both Barnum's Museum of the 1830s period and John W. Garrett's monumental Baltimore and Ohio building of the turn of the century occupied this site in turn until 1911 when Capt. Isaac Emerson, the Bromo-Seltzer king, put up his monument to Southern hospitality. The Emerson had a women-proof King Cole-type tavern, a marble lobby, and a general air of restraint, except for its French Renaissance flourishes at the roofline and a tiled roof garden for the tango set of World War I and the 1920s. One of the city's most glaring recent examples of the waste of a supremely solid building.

Built: 1911. Razed: 1971. Architect: Joseph E. Sperry.

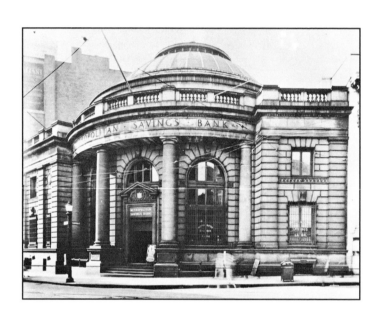

248

METROPOLITAN SAVINGS BANK

Southwest corner of Saratoga and Charles Streets

P ure Potsdam revival and perfectly suited to its setting, this small gem of a bank had a lovely rotunda floor that was one of the finest commercial interiors downtown. It was one of the earliest victims of Charles Center's grandeurs, perhaps 15 years too early to be sensibly incorporated into a sophisticated renewal plan.

Built: 1908. Razed: 1963. Architects: Parker, Thomas & Rice.

OLD SUN BUILDING

Southwest corner of Baltimore and Charles Streets

Probably the most imposing facade built downtown immediately after the great fire was the Baltimore *Sun* building that enriched the very heart of town for not quite six decades. With its baroque roofline and stirring colonnade, the *Sun*'s home office evoked the sort of international or Edwardian Fleet Street tone then being passionately sought by the proprietors. Vacated by the publishers on December 26, 1950, the *Sun* building succumbed to Charles Center clearance.

Built: 1906. Razed: 1964. Architects: Baldwin & Pennington.

252

COLONIAL TRUST COMPANY

6 West Saratoga Street

This elegant structure, probably the finest French Classic facade in the state, was one of those sacrificed for the Charles Center development. One of dozens of financial institutions in the city at the turn of the century, the Colonial was burned out of the Calvert building in 1904 and resettled north of the old fire zone.

Built: after 1904. Razed: 1964? Architects: Ellicott & Emmart.

NATIONAL EXCHANGE BANK

Liberty and Redwood Streets

This monumental little island structure was the centerpiece of the once grandly urban Hopkins Place neighborhood. The National Exchange Bank, chartered in 1865, catered to the area's wholesalers and its unique pediment was added to an older building that virtually filled its tiny wedge-shaped block. Magnificent Palladian windows with enormous cast iron grilles were architectural features of the rear elevations (not seen in photo). Built: about 1907. Razed: late 1950s. Architects: probably Ellicott & Emmart.

BAUERNSCHMIDT HOUSE

University Parkway and St. Paul Street

For about a half a century, this fine V-shaped home honored the southern entrance to the beautiful Guilford district. It was the home of the formidable Mrs. Marie Bauernschmidt, civic gadfly and heiress to a brewery fortune. A nondescript highrise apartment replaced the old mansion—luckily for everyone from the Mayor on down, *after* the death of Mrs. Bauernschmidt.

Built: 1907. Razed: early 1960s. Architects: Ellicott & Emmart.

WEST LEXINGTON STREET

The unit block west of North Charles Street

Old West Lexington was the 42nd Street of Baltimore in the golden days of Hollywood. The central marquee was the entrance to the great Wizard Theater, pulled down for Charles Center, along with its neighbor on the right, the exotically-named Blue Mouse. The street had a winding, intimate scale almost wholly gone from central Baltimore today.

Built: 1880-1920. Razed: early 1960s.

MARYLAND INSTITUTE SCHOOL OF ART AND DESIGN

Market Place at East Baltimore Street

An attractive design, at once staid and yet suggestive of eighteenth-century Paris, this handsome, barracks-like structure was part of a once fine, now almost gone ensemble of government market houses along the old Fallsway corridor. It was willfully destroyed by the city for a roads extension, just as the north harbor area was staging a comeback as a center for the arts and professional education.

Built: 1907. Razed: 1968. Architects: Simonson & Pietsch.

262

THE TOWER BUILDING

Baltimore Street at Guilford Avenue

Romance and early twentieth-century dreams are associated in this building, allowed to go to ruin slowly in its undesirable site on the edge of the city's raffish night club district. Prosperous Maryland Casualty Company created the place, with its tower and arcade, in the years after the 1904 fire. William Randolph Hearst, the newspaper czar, bought the building in 1923, but it was never occupied by a newspaper; vibration of the presses would have endangered the tower, legend relates. When completed it was, at 341 feet, the city's tallest structure, sporting a massive Seth Thomas clock with a 17-foot face and a public observatory at the 18th-story level with a "writing salon." For decades, a compact arcade that led through the building housed the Maryland bureau of the Associated Press. As is the case with many such losses, the present (1990) site is vacant. It had been sold to developers and the cash realized went to refund deposits of savings and loan customers victimized in a banking fraud case.

Built: 1910-12. Razed: 1986. Architects: Parker & Thomas.

THE ROYAL (DOUGLAS) THEATER

1329-33 Pennsylvania Avenue

A major stop on the jazz and big band circuit in its day, the Royal was also a sort of mecca for black artists. It had hosted Ella Fitzgerald, Billie Holiday, Louis Armstrong, and Duke Ellington during its heyday from the early 1920s until the end of World War II. The drastic clearance of lower Pennsylvania Avenue claimed it.

Built: 1921. Razed: 1971.

266

THE AUTOMOBILE CLUB
OF MARYLAND

Southeast corner of Mount Royal Avenue and Cathedral Street

This gemlike little building, only 53 by 83 feet square, hovered between Gothic Revival, Art Deco, and Louis Sullivan, but its small scale housed an auto agency (the Peerless), lavish AAA offices, and a third-floor auditorium. The AAA moved out in the late 1960s and the splendid little building, succumbing to the thing it was built to celebrate, became a parking lot!

Built: 1917. Razed: 1972. Architects: Wyatt & Nolting.

McCORMICK & COMPANY
BUILDING

Inner Harbor, 414 Light Street

This nine-story behemoth, the west harbor's most conspicuous landmark for nearly 70 years, came to grief at the hands of two of the largest Maryland-based corporations— The Rouse Company, which bought the property, and McCormick Tea and Spice Company, which created it in the 1920s and sold it along with more than $500 million in real estate. The design, an honest expression of advanced industrial planning for its era, was by a former B&O railroad engineering chief. Factory floors wafted cinnamon and other spice odors through the downtown area. An elaborate "Olde English" tea room and fake village street featured on one floor, very popular for civic events, was saved intact and relocated to the company's new headquarters in Sparks, Maryland. The old loft's replacement was the usual deadly parking lot, pending later construction.

Built: 1921. Razed: 1989. Architect: M.A. Long, Architects-Engineers.

Some Lesser Losses – An Epilogue

For every major architectural masterpiece that just isn't there anymore in and around Baltimore, many others of lesser note existed, structures that either were not up to the standard of surviving or demolished buildings of their type. They were important, nevertheless, for what they gave the city late in the last century and early in this one in terms of a patina, an echo, a voice of the past and evidence of mechanical skills of long ago.

From the earliest period was South Bond Street's Adam Boss house, a clapboard cottage of no great distinction except for age (circa 1710), possibly the oldest structure, period, in the immediate city area. Also ancient was the Carpet Loom building which survived into the telephone age (possibly about 1880), a picturesque ramble at Redwood and Liberty Streets (northwest corner) that went up in the 1740s soon after the city's chartering. Of about the same period were the original structures of St. Paul's Episcopal Church, incinerated in 1786 at North Charles and Saratoga Streets, still the parish's home. The William Lux mansion (circa 1750) at West Franklin and Pine Streets lasted into the photographic age and was razed about 1890 for row house development. Romance sometimes played a role in homes that were once there, but no more. The alliance between wealthy Baltimore beauty Betsy Patterson and her one-time husband, Jerome Bonaparte, was remembered by locals for a mansion in the 1100 block of Winchester Street—a late Georgian building with an unusual pediment rising above the roofline and an arched entry flanked by window lights. Up until 1907, passersby could see the tiny but elegant estate of the French consul, the Chevalier D'Annemours of the Napoleonic era. Also long forgotten is the west end estate of "Harlem," near the present intersection of Fulton Avenue and Mount Street, a big and boxy Georgian manse of about 1789, home of one of the city's first art collectors. The chevalier's residence was at East North Avenue and Harford Road.

Though they are missed by few, many of the blue-collar houses of the 1820s and 1830s were, to their occupants, a step up in the world. On Baltimore's near east and west sides, these structures vanished wholesale in the clearance of the "urban renewal" years. Pine Street and an adjoining twin, Pearl, were major working class survivals, a lifestyle preserved in hundreds of restorations elsewhere, including Federal Hill and Fells Point.

By contrast, historical associations can save a building, but it did nothing for the old Murdock mansion at 15 East Pleasant Street in the "old court" district when a parking lot became a burning necessity about 1935. In 1824, Lafayette had attended a locally famous ball on the third floor of this huge home, later famous as the clinic of Dr. James Smith, a vaccination pioneer. Two other famous victims were near neighbors of each other in Court Square. These were the Greek Revival Williams townhouse at North Calvert and Lexington Streets and the Reverdy Johnson mansion on the northeast corner of Calvert and Fayette Streets, a Union military headquarters during the Civil War.

Country buildings, on the other hand, had a better chance of survival than townhouses on expensive lots. Gothic and Italian designs of the nineteenth century sometimes escaped destruction. The big, high-ceilinged buildings done in board and batten and rough-cut stone, or a mixture of both, satisfied the Victorian craving for the picturesque. One excellent sample that did not survive was the graceful, Gothic rectory of Redeemer Episcopal Church, razed in the 1950s to provide land for the building of a new sanctuary. The rectory dated from the Civil War period. Free-standing Victorian mansions or those of the later Beaux Arts period proved harder to maintain and usually sported a heavier tax burden. Two examples were the Epstein mansion, a superb, if somewhat cold mockup of high Philadelphia Georgian architecture and the nearby Brooks mansion. Both overlooked Druid Lake and the park. The Epstein home needed only a $50,000 fixup to survive the 1950s, a careless decade. The Brooks mansion, "Cloverdale," on Eutaw Place extended, was an amusing melange of Italian cupola, southern verandah, and mansard roof with a heroic Greek pediment to round out the mixture. It disappeared about 1906. A rather more unified loss was "Nacirema," in the Green Spring valley north of town, built in the 1850s by Alexander Stump in Italian villa styling and razed about 1926. (The land on which it stood became the setting for another Italian villa, home of world famous Met soprano Rosa Ponselle.) The largest of all the Tuscan-inspired houses of the earlier period, "Guilford," was destroyed when the deluxe intown mansion settlement was created early in the twentieth century and named after the estate.

Some historic losses are special cases unto themselves; others are simply the result of residential growth. Baltimore built lean and elegant in both brick and timber as the eighteenth century waned. A 1795 treasure was the Kirby family mansion in what had been countryside at Fulton Avenue and Mosher Streets until the thundering crash of row house mansions crept westward in the 1870s and 1880s. Also a victim, but much later, in the 1960s, was "Willowbrook," the fine 1799 estate of the Smith and Donnell families at Hollins and Mount Streets on the west side. Its superb oval drawing room (saved and recreated at the Baltimore Museum of Art) has the same echoes of Federal period elegance that also survives in William Thornton's Octagon House in Washington. A convent razing claimed what survived of the Willowbrook original fabric.

Baltimore has had relatively hard luck with its famous hostelries, which seemed not to have had staying power, despite furious popularity. The Fountain Inn, the Eutaw House, Barnum's, and the Emerson, all were famous hostelries in their day; so too were the vast Carrollton, an enormous Light Street ornament just below Baltimore, done in the best French Empire-U.S. Grant architecture but turned into a cinder by the 1904 fire, and the Armistead, facing City Hall, consumed by the municipal employees union, which wanted to build itself a rather more elaborate headquarters close to the seat of government. The Armistead, earlier called the Raleigh, on the corner of East Fayette and Holliday Streets, was perhaps the only building ever done in the city that mimicked Italian Alpine styling.

Adaptive use has saved, and also altered, many urban structures. A number of the huge townhouses built in the Mt. Vernon district in the nineteenth century within a generation or two became institutionalized as schools, rectories or clubs for the elite. Among these was the Edgeworth school (Madame Lefebre's) with a strong southern patronage for 30 years on West Franklin Street.

Street widenings were another cause of institutional razings, and the Charles Street Methodist Church, a noble Ionic temple built in 1844 that straddled the steep Charles Street hill near Baltimore Street, was one such loss about 1885. Luckily, the porticoed, Greek Revival-type church still has a half-dozen or so prototypes in the old city limits, notably on the west side. Also a victim of street enlargement was fashionable Lehmann's Hall on North Howard Street, utilitarian outside to the point of ugliness but the site of aristocratic balls of the bon ton for 40 years. When Cathedral Street was extended to give direct access to the downtown area, the A.S. Abell townhouse, with elegantly bowed gable ends, was demolished on Saratoga Street, a third victim of street engineering.

Like their more comfy counterparts the country villas

and homey row house mansions, institutional villas followed the current rage for the picturesque through the nineteenth century. Downtown buildings were rarely masterpieces, but the banking house of John S. Gittings, done in the 1870s at Guilford Avenue and East Fayette Street, was a controlled masterpiece of elegant Italian spirited design, knocked over about 1940. Its sweeping, double outside staircase was a graceful amenity that echoed a more gracious age.

Relatively few Baltimore buildings have adopted the late Tudor or Jacobean style of the sixteenth and seventeenth centuries, a mode that has left some landmarks on at least 50 percent of U.S. college campuses. One that did was the old City College high school building of 1874 with corbelled bay oriel windows and a handsome English tower. Apparently, it was built on less than perfect foundations for tunneling under its Howard Street site weakened the walls and it was razed during the 1890s. An unusual small trend in building that left some specimens put up largely in the 1880s and 90s might be called the "eyebrow" school of architecture. It is typified by overhangs of rooflines that gave windows a peek-a-boo effect—a sort of witch's hat approach to architecture. Such was the notoriously busy Claremont Hotel at the Union Stockyards in west Baltimore, a destination stop for shippers, cattlemen and railroad-borne drummers of the late nineteenth and early twentieth centuries.

Municipal architecture before World War I was nothing if not substantial and sheer hell to demolish. Among the noble victims of the road craze of the 1950s and 1960s was the city's Mount Royal pumping station, a humongous essay in masonry designed by Henry Brauns, originally thought of as an ornament to the city's largest park entrance at North Avenue and McMechen Street. Substantial, too, in the masonry manner was the unlovely but practical Union (or Pennsylvania) Station, replaced by a $2 million Beaux Arts extravaganza (recently restored) after 70 years of intensive use. A fine small specimen of masonry succumbed in the 1960s, the Hopkins Place Savings Bank of 1893 that had survived the fire but could not survive redevelopment plans for the west end center. An even finer structure of somewhat later date, the old Union Trust Company building at Baltimore and Light Streets was also ripped down in the 1980s for a bank high-rise construction.

The impression continues to persist that all the buildings taken in 1904 by the fire were destroyed. The fact is that a number of major ones survived and were rebuilt. They included the magnificent masonry Equitable Building still standing in Court Square and the Continental Trust Company building on the southeast corner of Baltimore and Calvert Streets. A third fire survival was the Calvert building, an engaging early highrise of 1900 once packed with the elite of the legal profession. It was razed for a parking lot (and a later highrise) 70 years after the fire gutted it.

It is surprising that Baltimore, except for its very earliest years, has always had a museum or two. One of the earliest, and by all odds the most colorful, was the Baltimore Museum at East Baltimore and Calvert Streets. The 1825 building went up in flames in 1873 but it had a showy facade with a columned portico topped by a huge lunette and an elegant railing at the roofline. The Baltimore Museum could lay claim to being the city's first multi-purpose center, for within its cavernous depths it could house a theater, circus acts, animal relics, a lottery office, stationery stores, art shows, plays and concerts. From 1846 until 1851 it was operated by the legendary P.T. Barnum. Such non-masterpieces of architecture perhaps reveal more about the social life and strife of old times than the surviving memorials of grandeur.

In any event, after a fairly decent 1970s record beating back destruction of landmarks, the 1980s proved to be a disastrous decade for older sections of the city's downtown. Escalating values called for a recycling of land, which investors vigorously pursued. Scarcely able to resist were local authorities, a slack administration and the pliable standards of the city's Commission on Historic Preservation, not to mention the indifference of Baltimore's government and its housing officers. "If you want a parking lot, buy a Baltimore building," was virtually the rallying cry of outsiders and a few insiders as well. The city's financial policies worked to their advantage, seldom, if ever, requiring performance bonds on approved building plans. This permitted acres of sleazy takeovers by speculators and projects that never projected anything but parking lot (and building) revenues. The oldest of these con games dates back to the late 1960s and the destruction of Robert Mills' "Waterloo Row" landmark of 1815 (see page 70), where a megablock dream of downtown housing took 20 years to realize and free the area from a devastating parking lot scar.

Acknowledgments

This study owes just as much to the historic print and photo resources of metropolitan Baltimore as it does to any author. Help on a broad front was furnished for months by the Enoch Pratt Free Library, with special thanks due the late Dr. Morgan Pritchett, former head of the Maryland Department of the Pratt, and Robert Stevens, assistant head of the department, for their unfailing expertise. Other essential material was contributed by the Baltimore *Sunpapers* through Clement G. Vitek and his staff, and by the Maryland Historical Society, where Paula Velthuys, print and photo librarian, uncovered little-known graphics. Single images, without which this book would have been incomplete, were graciously furnished by the Maryland Commission on Afro-American Culture and History, the Methodist Historical Society, and Baltimore architect Alexander S. Cochran. Unpublished material of great value was contributed by the University of Maryland Baltimore County through Thomas E. Beck, curator of photography, and by Ross J. Kelbaugh, Pikesville photohistorian and collector. Frederick N. Rasmussen, editor of *Menckeniana* magazine, was a valued research associate during the book's preparation. John Maclay collected much additional material and produced the first edition. Since publication, several architectural scholars have assisted with verifications of dates and, most notably, attributions to architects. In this regard we are grateful to Dr. Robert L. Alexander of the University of Iowa; Randolph W. Chalfant, of Baltimore; and Carlos P. Avery, of Rockville.

This second edition was born of a partnership between the Historic Baltimore Society and the Institute for Publications Design at the University of Baltimore. The book was designed and produced by Marsha Miller, a graduate student in the Publications Design program, under the direction of Professor Bert Smith. The University of Baltimore Graphics Lab provided computers and space to work for a significant portion of the project. Cass Tyson assisted with desktop publishing production.

For all their assistance finding and reprinting photos for the second edition, thanks are due to: Averil Kadis, The Enoch Pratt Free Library; Margaret Welsh and Jeff Goldman, The Maryland Historical Society; Jim Lynn, McCormick & Company; and Mary Markey, The Peale Museum.

This book was produced using Ventura Publisher. The text is set in Palatino, and chapter headings are in Palatino Cursive.

Illustration Credits

Index

Page numbers in boldface refer to photographs.

About the Author

Carleton Jones is a Baltimore journalist and lecturer who has been writing on Maryland topics for three decades in local and state publications. A 1949 graduate in history of the University of Missouri, he joined the Baltimore *Sun* in 1952. From 1968 until 1976 he wrote weekly commentary on local and state development and architectural preservation, and he won the national newsfeature award for 1972 of the National Association of Real Estate Editors. He also has been an award winner four times in the annual A.D. Emmart competitions for Maryland writing in the humanities.

Mr. Jones has lectured before the Society of Colonial Wars, the Maryland Historical Society, and the Women's Civic League. His special field is the graphic and architectural heritage of Maryland's Civil War period. He is the author of *Maryland: A Picture History* (Bodine & Associates, Inc., 1976) and co-author of *Baltimore: A Picture History*, jointly published by Maclay & Associates and Bodine & Associates, Inc. His most recent volume is *Streetwise Baltimore*, an illustrated history of Baltimore streets and street names published in 1991 by Bonus Books, Inc. In preparation is a history of the War of 1812 from the Chesapeake Bay and Baltimore viewpoint.